The CIA Pattern

Transform Your Life With Your Inner "Dream Team"

NLP Mastery Series

By

Sarah Carson and Shawn Carson

Changing Mind Publishing
New York, NY

Changing Mind Publishing
New York, NY

The CIA Pattern
NLP Mastery Series
©Copyright 2016 Sarah Carson and Shawn Carson and
Changing Mind Publishing

**For further information, please contact Changing Mind
Publishing, 545 8th Avenue, Suite 930, New York, NY 10018**

Cover Design by Richie Williamson
Photography courtesy of Caroline Bergonzi
Editing by Wendell Anderson

Contents

Introduction   5

Chapter 1: The History of the CIA Pattern   8

Chapter 2: Overview of the CIA Pattern   15

Chapter 3: The Neuroscience of the CIA Pattern   22

Chapter 4: Inside the CIA Toolbox   37

Chapter 5: Creating your Council   48

Chapter 6: Creating the Council Chamber   61

Chapter 7: Introducing Council Members to the Chamber 70

Chapter 8: The First Council Meeting   77

Chapter 9: Interacting with Your Council   84

Chapter 10: Dream Incubation   94

Chapter 11: NLP, Hypnosis, and the CIA Pattern   103

Chapter 12: The BEAT Pattern   109

Chapter 13: Tree of Life   122

Chapter 14: The Perfect Coach Pattern   128

Chapter 15: NLP Disney Pattern   133

Chapter 16: The Polar Sphinx Pattern   138

Conclusion: Other Ways to Use Your CIA   144

Appendix I: Using the CIA Pattern to Write This Book 149

Appendix II: Shawn's Original Council of Advisers   182

Introduction

Have you ever wished you could create like Leonardo Da Vinci, have the business acumen of Richard Branson, the compassion of the Dalai Lama, or the brilliant mind of Nikola Tesla; or maybe the determination of an Olympic athlete, the flair of a renowned designer, or the strategic ability of a chess grand master?

Have you ever wondered what it might be like to sit down and chat with Elizabeth I, seek advice from Abraham Lincoln, or ask for guidance from Nelson Mandela? Imagine having coffee with Babe Ruth, sitting for down for tea with Jane Austen, or shooting the breeze with Wolverine. Who in the world would you most like to meet and receive insight and guidance from? Who would have a place on your personal "dream team" of experts to guide you through life?

Within this book, you will learn the hypnotic and neurolinguistic programming (NLP) principles that will allow you do just that. These principles are the secret steps to a pattern used by many of the world's most successful people, the CIA Pattern. This pattern will show you how to tap into the power of your unconscious mind and draw from it infinite amounts of wisdom, inspiration, and success.

Richard Bandler and John Grinder developed neurolinguistic programming in the 1970s. Its origins can be traced back to 1975 to the publication of Bandler and Grinder's two-volume book *The Structure of Magic*. However, the principles of NLP were being used in the field of personal development as far back as the 1930s at least. In 1937, a writer named Napoleon Hill published a book that can still be read today as a classic of personal development and NLP even though it predates the birth of NLP by almost 40 years. This book is called *Think and Grow Rich*. Tucked away at the back of the book is an amazing description of one of Mr. Hill's practices. When I (Shawn) read through this technique, although the description is not detailed in the way an NLP pattern would be, my jaw literally dropped at the perfect combination of several NLP and hypnosis techniques.

We have borrowed this technique from Mr. Hill and have updated it to include specific underlying NLP and hypnosis patterns and a description of exactly how this technique may be applied in practice.

We have to warn you, though, practicing this technique on a regular basis WILL transform your life in totally revolutionary ways!

The idea of a council of advisers is not new. Kings and queens, dukes and princes, and other people of power have gathered the wise and the good to advise them on policy of state. Universities and other places of learning have gathered the leading experts in their fields to generate new ideas and theories. Companies have gathered experienced businessmen and businesswomen on boards of directors to advise them. Many famous and successful people have gathered a council of advisers, and their success has reflected the combined wisdom of this group. The people on a real-life council of advisers may be your mentors, colleagues, or simply friends.

We're not sure where the idea of a purely mental council of advisers came from. We do know that people have consulted spirit guides for centuries. We will discuss Napoleon Hill's work on the council of advisers later. What is new are the NLP tools that allow us to model the excellence of others, and the hypnotic tools that allow us to identify with these individuals on a much deeper level. Combining these tools with Napoleon Hill's ideas can create amazing and thoroughly transformative experience, which you are now ready to begin.

About This book

We use the terms *advisers* and *council members* interchangeability throughout this book. This book was written with the help of a Council of Inner Advisers (CIA) and, being someone dedicated to practicing what I preach, I (Sarah) decided to create a CIA specifically designed to assist and guide me through the writing of this book. My writing council had six members and, over the months, I frequently met with them, using self-hypnosis to ask for suggestions, seek guidance, run ideas past them, and consolidate my thoughts. I documented my experiences with them and have included extracts throughout this book as specific examples of various aspects and techniques used within the CIA Pattern. I have included the full transcript of the meetings at the end of this book. Hopefully, you will find this useful, informative, and interesting!

While primarily a personal change pattern, the CIA Pattern can also be used to work with clients. A background and training in hypnosis and NLP is needed for this type of work. With this in mind, we have also included transcripts from client sessions as examples of how this pattern can be used for deep transformational change work with clients.

Warning: Do not use this pattern if you are under the care of a mental health professional.

Chapter 1: The History of the CIA Pattern

The Royal Council

Councils have been around for probably as long since humans gained the ability to speak. Originally, no doubt, tribal councils would have been called on the collective wisdom of the oldest, wisest, most experienced, skilled, and cunning minds of the village to decide where to stay, where to hunt, and if and when to move on. As tribes turned into kingdoms, the role of the royal council was to provide wise advice to the king himself, who would execute that advice.

To examine the role of the royal council, let's take a look at perhaps the best known example, the synedrion of one of the world's greatest rulers, Alexander the Great. Alexander used not only a royal council to advise him but also Deep Trance Identification to draw on the inspiration of the legendary hero Achilles!

Before we get to Alexander's synedrion, it may be worthwhile examining how Alexander's father, Philip, first formed the synedrion—although for a very different purpose.

Philip II of Macedon (the father of Alexander the Great) proved himself the strongest leader in classical Greece. After unifying

Macedonia and making himself king in 359 BCE, Philip turned his attention to the wider world. The other Greek city-states, particularly Athens, feared that Philip would conquer the rest of Greece. However, Philip had bigger plans than the mere conquest of Greece, plans that required the Greeks as willing allies, not a conquered people living under the yoke of a tyrant.

As a result, Philip created an organization that united the Greek city-states in the League of Corinth, a sort of ancient United Nations. Corinth was a Greek city-state that, although nominally independent, in reality Philip controlled. It even had a Macedonian garrison stationed there to provide the military muscle for Philip. To politically control the league, Philip designed a council of representatives called the *synedrion* (from the Greek for "those who sit together") from all the states in the league. The synedrion was empowered to deliberate and decide on actions to be taken in the event of the peace threatened by internal or external enemies. After the decisions were made, their execution lay with Philip as *hegemon*, or leader. Philip's leverage with various Greek city-states, and control over Corinth, gave him de facto control over the synedrion, which was, consequently, less an advisory body and more a tool of control.

Philip planned to leverage his effective control and use the League of Corinth to attack the Persian Empire, the most powerful military force in the world at that time. Unfortunately for Philip, fate had a different end in mind: he was assassinated before his plans came to fruition, leaving his son Alexander to take up where he had left off. The rest is history. Alexander went on to conquer the Persian Empire and lands beyond even into India. Greece became but a small part of his mighty empire.

So what happened to the synedrion, the body Philip had set up to control Greece? Surely, Alexander, the headstrong conqueror of the world, had no need for advice. To find the answer, we have to travel back to Alexander's childhood as heir to the throne of Macedonia.

During Alexander's childhood, Philip hired a number of tutors for the young Alexander, including the philosopher Aristotle. Alexander's favorite tutor was Lysimachus. Not much is known about Lysimachus except that he encouraged Alexander to play a game whereby Alexander became Achilles, the Greek hero of the Trojan Wars. Indeed, it is said that Alexander modeled himself after Achilles for the rest of his life.

Following his conquest of Persia, Alexander transformed the synedrion into a true advisory council. Little survives of the actual workings of the synedrion, but two important principles, on which the workings of the synedrion were based, remain.

The first of these principles is *parrhesia*, meaning "freedom of speech." Everyone was free, indeed expected, to express their opinion fully, openly, and honestly during meetings of the synedrion. In other forums, those with unpopular opinions might be concerned about being viewed negatively by speaking out, but in the synedrion everyone was free to express their views without censorship.

The second principle of the synedrion was called *isegoria*, meaning "equality of word." *Isegoria* means that each synedrion member's opinion was considered as valuable as anyone else's. Even Alexander's opinions carried no more weight within the synedrion than others' opinions. *Isegoria* allowed an issue to be viewed from different perspectives; for example, a decision on whether to go to war might be considered by philosophers, statesmen, poets, and soldiers within the synedrion, each with his own perspective.

Now that we have at least one example of how a council or advisers works in practice, we examine how Napoleon Hill turned this idea into a technique for personal transformation.

Napoleon Hill

The great self-help guru Napoleon Hill realized that not everyone has the luxury of being Alexander the Great, with the ability to call on the greatest minds in his empire to join his synedrion.

So, instead, Hill formed his own mental council, known as the Cabinet of Invisible Counselors. Hill ran his cabinet for a number of years using nine members: Ralph Waldo Emerson, Thomas Paine, Thomas Edison, Charles Darwin, Abraham Lincoln, Luther Burbank, Napoleon Bonaparte, Henry Ford, and Dale Carnegie. Each member was carefully chosen to bring certain skills, insights, or character strengths to Hill's cabinet.

Each night, before he slept, Hill met with his cabinet. Describing this procedure Hill said, "Just before going to sleep at night, I would shut my eyes and see, in my imagination, this group of men seated with me around my council table."

Hill described his purpose in this exercise of imagination as "to rebuild [his] character so it would represent a composite of the characters of my imaginary characters." Hill presented his technique in his classic 1937 book *Think and Grow Rich*. The technique is presented almost as an afterthought toward the end of the book. It is said that Hill considered leaving it out of the book entirely in case his descriptions led people to consider him insane. Hill stated in *Think and Grow Rich*, "This is the first time I have had the courage to mention this." The story goes that his editors also felt the need to remove certain sections. This may seem a little far-fetched to us, but Hill stated, "These meetings became so realistic that I became fearful of their consequences and discontinued them for [six] months. The experiences were so uncanny, I was afraid I would lose sight of the fact the meetings were [imaginary]."

It is worthwhile exploring what disturbed Hill so much, and what brought him back to meeting with his council after he had discontinued it. What disturbed Hill was that the members of his cabinet appeared to behave independently of what Hill himself expected. For example, "Lincoln developed the habit of always being late [to cabinet meetings]." In the same way, each member developed his own curious characteristics of behavior that seemingly had little to do with the business of the cabinet.

Having discontinued the meetings with his cabinet, one night Hill received a visitor in his bedroom—none other than Abraham Lincoln himself. Lincoln said that the world had need of Hill's ideas and encouraged him to continue his explorations. As a result, Hill reconvened his cabinet. When they appeared, they stood at their places around the table and Lincoln proposed a toast: "To a friend who has returned to the fold."

The incredible aptitude of the human imagination to create a life-like experience is perhaps less surprising to modern readers used to 3-D IMAX movies and ultrarealistic video games. However, it is a reminder of the power of the CIA Pattern and why it should not be undertaken by anyone with psychological problems or otherwise under the care of a mental health professional.

Hill's technique is simple and powerful and forms the foundation of our CIA Pattern described later in this book. Meeting with his cabinet within his imagination, Hill would pose a specific question, and as he imagined his cabinet discussing the issue, he would drift off to sleep. When he woke in the morning, he would more often than not have solutions to the question posed. His cabinet members also suggested ideas to Hill that were unrelated to the questions raised. As time went on, and Hill continued to work with his cabinet, he expanded its membership to more than 50.

So how did Hill himself explain how his Cabinet of Invisible Advisers worked? Remarkably, the answer was received from Thomas Edison who arrived at one council meeting ahead of the other members and laid out this theory. Edison explained the very secret of life, that there were intelligent entities, or "units," that group together around a common core or set or principles. But within that group were differences of opinion (just as the members of Hill's cabinet had differences of opinions). The cabinet process invited in units aligned with Hill's values and goals.

The most remarkable thing is that Thomas Edison was still alive at that time, and Hill made an appointment to see him. When Hill had told Edison (the real Edison!) about his experience with the imaginary Edison, Edison "smiled broadly, and said, 'Your dream was more a reality than you may imagine.'"

If you think that Hill's (or Edison's) explanation is a little far-fetched, we ask you to hold your opinion until you have read about Michael Graziano's work in the chapter on neuroscience.

The CIA Lab

We love to apply neurolinguistic programming (NLP) and hypnosis principles to new areas of thought and run "labs" for our students that demonstrate a new or classical, but rarely used, patterns for them to explore. We based one such lab on Hill's Cabinet of Invisible Counselors Pattern. Now I (Shawn) did not care for the word *cabinet* (which sounds to me like a cupboard), so, wanting to add a certain intrigue to the title of the lab, I called it the CIA Pattern, for Council of Invisible Advisers.

We took the technique that Hill had outlined in *Think and Grow Rich* and turned it into a workshop where students would choose council members, construct their meeting space, hold their first meeting, and use NLP and hypnosis tools and techniques to use their council effectively. Needless to say, the lab was a great hit, and Sarah and I decided to write a book to present the detailed techniques to the world. Thankfully, we have finally got around to that task!

Deep Trance Identification

Within this book, you will see us refer to Deep Trance Identification (DTI). Deep Trance Identification involves "becoming" another person rather than simply dialoguing with that person as in the CIA Pattern. We don't directly use DTI within the CIA Pattern, but we do use some of the DTI tools to flesh out the characters and skills of members of the council.[1]

---

[1] For more information on DTI, please refer to the book *Deep Trance Identification* by Shawn Carson, Jess Marion, with John Overdurf

Chapter 2: Overview of the CIA Pattern

In this chapter, we provide a brief overview of the CIA Pattern. Later in the book, we discuss each step more fully; however, we think it a good idea to give you the basic pattern in its entirety first. Of course, there are numerous adaptations and various ways this pattern can be used, and we share some of these in later chapters too.

You can think of the basic CIA Pattern in six easy steps:

1. Creating your council
2. Creating the council chamber
3. Introducing council members to the chamber
4. Holding your first meeting
5. Interacting with your council
6. Sleeping on it

Step 1: Creating Your Council

The first step is to select the people you would like to be a part of your council. You have a vast array of people to choose from. You can select anyone, living or dead, famous or infamous, personally known to you or a famous icon. You can select fictional characters from movies, books, TV programs, comic strips, or literature. You can choose friends or foes, good guys or bad guys, Cleopatra or your next-door neighbor, Albert Einstein or Lassie the dog. It really doesn't matter who you choose as long as you know that each person you select brings a certain characteristic and trait that you admire or feel you could use more of. Select people who you feel can bring worthwhile advice, tough love or wisdom. One interesting factor is that you really don't need to know a tremendous amount about the person you select (although it helps if you do) for that person to be a wonderful council member. As long as you have a strong reason for inviting each one to your council, that is usually enough!

You may have different advisers for specific projects (see Sarah's account of her CIA for book writing in Appendix 1) as well as a general CIA for life. One simple way to select members is to make a list of people you admire and consciously select from that list. Another method is to make the list but allow your unconscious mind to choose; simply see who shows up in your council chamber! Either way can work, and it is always interesting when someone unexpected arrives for a meeting!

We give further guidance on the conscious and unconscious methods of selection later in this book.

To truly make this a group of people who will provide good counsel and advise, we strongly recommend diversifying your council members. When you select members for your general council, it's not the best idea to select all creative types or all young people or all men. Make your council a good balance of attributes, gender, age, and abilities. Of course, each individual is a complex human, and even though you may have selected someone for one specific trait or ability, it is very likely that person will have so much more to offer than that one aspect of himself.

For example: Let's say you have chosen the pop star Madonna to be on your council for her ability to think creatively and to move with new and upcoming trends. Yet I have to think that Madonna is also a very astute businesswoman and may bring some aspects of this to your council in addition.

We also suggest that you don't pick people who are too much like you! The purpose of the CIA is to develop a council to broaden and expand, to advise in new ways, and to help you to develop new ways of thinking and of being. Simply filling your council with "mini-me's" is less likely to achieve this effect.

In short, when selecting your advisers, keep in mind to have a broad and diverse range of inner guides.

Step 2: Creating the Council Chamber

Once you have selected members for your council, you will need a specific place for them to meet. You may already have a special place you go to in your mind for self-hypnosis, meditation, or relaxation, and using this place is perfectly fine. Alternatively, you may wish to create a space specifically designed for your council. Either way works perfectly—this is simply a matter of personal choice. One thing I will say is this: be comfortable with the idea that your council chamber is very likely to change over time. Given this, it is a great idea to have one chamber, an aleph point, a place that is the starting point that you can access easily in your mind's eye. This will help to focus and ground your experience.

Again, you can use any place real or imagined, a place that you have visited, would love to visit, or one that your unconscious mind creates for you. Many of us have either real or imagined places where we feel deeply relaxed, entirely comfortable, and at ease. A place where we feel or have felt openness, a spiritual connection, or a self-knowing. Your council chamber doesn't have to be a traditional room; it can be inside or outside, a quiet hillside or garden, or even a bustling café. You can allow your unconscious mind to create the perfect place for your council to gather. We suggest that wherever you decide to meet, make the seating/standing arrangement equal. By this we mean that it is a good idea to have seats at the same height and arranged in such a way that everyone can be equally heard and included.

Remember the principle of *isegoria*, the "equality of word," from chapter 1.

Step 3: Introducing Council Members to the Chamber

Once you have established a council chamber, ask each member of your Inner Council to enter the chamber. We suggest you do this individually and take time to welcome each person to the chamber and to the council.

In trance, simply call members, by name, and invite them into the chamber. Notice how they walk, enter the chamber, what they are wearing, and other points about them. This helps to establish the visualization and create a deeper rapport with each of them. Welcome them as you would welcome anyone to your home, and thank them for agreeing to be a member of this group. Take some time to explain the purpose of this specific council group, and explain the reason you have selected them specifically to be part of your CIA.

Now, begin to show them around the council chamber. Ask each member if there is anything he would like to add or change in the room. You may be wonderfully surprised at the suggestions they make—from the fairly mundane ("I think we could use a whiteboard over in this corner") to the more elaborate ideas ("How about we knock down this wall and create an open space leading to a large patio with a fountain?") As all of this is an inner construct for you, feel free to alter your space. Be aware that sometimes your council members may disagree about the meeting space and you will have to have a meeting to discuss how to accommodate everyone's personal taste and suggestions.

This is also a wonderful opportunity to set up individual spaces where you can meet one on one with each member. Once you have introduced a member to the space and that person has made suggestions and recommendations, ask each person where she would like to have private time with you. At this point, you can allow your unconscious mind to create the perfect place. This space may be attached in some way to the initial meeting space, for example, an additional room within the house, or maybe entirely separate from the house.

Once you have welcomed your council members individually; thanked them for their participation; explained the specific character trait, skill, or ability you have selected them for; made any modifications to the space; and created a private space for one-on-one conversations, it is time for the first group meeting.

Step 4: Holding the First Meeting

At this first meeting, you may wish to take time to introduce the purpose of creating this specific council to its members. You may have created a council for a particular task; for example, you may have a council to advise you on taking the next step in your career, or a council for achieving a specific goal. You may have a more general archetype council that will become your standard "go-to" guys when seeking advice. Whatever the purpose of the council, take time to clearly outline this for all the members.

Once this is done, we suggest you introduce all the members to one another. You can take the lead here as the chairperson and introduce each person, or you may wish to ask each person to introduce herself or himself. Of course, there are other possibilities here too. I'm sure you have attended courses and meetings where there has been a meet and mingle, maybe a set time where you were asked to meet everyone in the room, or you meet everyone and then in a group setting introduce someone other than yourself. As chairperson, you decide the best way for your group to meet. Usually at the first meeting, I have found it easier to ask each individual to spend a few moments introducing himself or herself and to explain why each has been selected and what each hopes to bring to the council. There will always be time for a cheese-and-wine/meet-and-greet hour later, possibly on the patio by the fountain!

Step 5: Using the Council

Once the council and the meeting space have been established and each individual is introduced, it's time to begin to use the council. This can be a continuation of the initial meeting, or it may take place at a different time. Whenever you have a specific question, something you would like advise on, or need to run some ideas by your group of masterminds, that is the time to ask your CIA to convene. Simply allow yourself to go into trance, take yourself to your council chamber, and ask the members to appear—or they may well already be in place. When all members are in attendance, you can pose your questions or ideas and ask for advice and feedback. As in any regular meeting, you may ask one particular person, ask each in turn, or open the question to all in attendance for a group discussion. However you decide to run the meeting is perfectly correct for you.

Of course, there are additional methods for accessing the wisdom of your council. You may wish to do some automatic writing or journaling whilst in your meeting, ask your members to write or draw something for you, or create a story or metaphor. You can hold individual meetings or smaller group meetings, or ask another member of the council to be the chairperson for the meeting. The possibilities are endless and the potential vast!

Step 6: Sleeping on It

Sleeping on it is one of the most important pieces of the CIA Pattern. Traditionally called dream incubation, this is when we sleep, we dream, and when we dream, our mind puts all the learnings and knowledge from that day into place for us and makes sense of our experiences. We explain dream incubation in much more detail in a later chapter, but suffice it to say we can use dream incubation either to solidify an earlier CIA meeting or even for the meeting to take place inside a dream. You see, it's almost like planting a seed of an idea and allowing the unconscious mind/dream experience to utilize the Council of Inner Advisers to meet and discuss whilst we are sleeping.

As you fall asleep, you can go to the meeting chamber and assemble the council and ask a specific question. The unconscious mind is now directionalized to dream an answer or solution, a suggestion or idea for you to utilize. You may or may not be consciously aware of the dream upon awakening (as with any dream). However, you may have a moment of clarity, a thought may pop into your head, or a bright idea might occur the following days that could be a solution to your question.

We have given a brief outline of the basic Council of Inner Advisers Pattern here. In the following chapters, we go into further detail and deepen your understanding and broaden your scope for using this pattern.

Chapter 3: The Neuroscience of the CIA Pattern

In this chapter, we highlight some of the neuroscientific research that can provide a deeper understanding of how the mind works when using the CIA Pattern.

Over the past few years, there has been a tremendous amount of new neuroscience research that informs our practice as coaches/hypnotists and change-workers. Even if this is not your field of study or profession, this information will still have a profound effect on your understanding of how we function as humans.

Neuroscience includes the study of how our daily experiences and self-directed attention, like hypnosis, can affect the physical structure of our brain. Having this information allows us to understand more deeply the work we do as change-workers and as practitioners of personal development and self-improvement.

It was once thought that once we reached a certain age, our brain function and the number of neurons and neural connections we had would begin to diminish. This idea has now been proven incorrect. We now understand that the brain continues to generate new cells, make new connections, and create new neural pathways throughout our lives. The brain is constantly changing, rewiring, and adapting. This process begins in utero. This process is called *neuroplasticity* and is the foundation of the neuroscientific research that we cover within this book.

Let's do a brief thought experiment here. Take a moment and point to your brain. ... Now point to your mind.

Did you point to almost the same place? Maybe you pointed to your head in response to the question about the location of your brain and then waved your arms in an all-inclusive gesture to indicate your mind.

Most people are pretty much aware that the mind, attention, and the ability to think are different from the physical structure of the brain. But did you know that your mind can, in fact, alter your brain?

As an organ in your body, your brain has certain functions. The two main functions of the organ called your brain are to:

1. Learn things as efficiently and quickly as possible either by repetition or through the intensity of the experience
2. Create automatic programs by consolidating these learnings

This is how we learn! By repeating an activity, it eventually becomes part of your automatic ability, like tying your shoelaces. Think about it: Most of us as some early point in our lives had to learn to tie our shoes. I certainly remember fumbling with the laces and making numerous mistakes, unaware at the time that each attempt (whether successful or not) was creating more dexterity and a "muscle memory" in my fingers. After a time, however, tying my shoelaces has become an automatic program, so automatic that as an adult I barely have to think about it.

Now, the neurons in the brain are much like the muscles in our bodies. Through training, the neurons in the brain will become more coordinated, stronger, and more efficient. They will fire more effectively and be more sensitive to "firing off" at the correct time.

In fact, your brain has been rewiring itself even whilst you have been reading this book. As you move forward though the ideas and views in this book, as you try out the exercises, consider the ideas and play along with the mind games. Your brain is creating, conditioning, and strengthening the neural pathways and connections around the concept of the CIA Pattern. The more you engage in these practices and exercises, the more your brain is learning to quickly and easily make this process automatic. This means that when the time is right for you to visualize, go into a light trance, picture the members of your CIA in your mind's eye and interact with them. However you decide to engage with your CIA, the easier and smoother it will be. So take a moment and thank your brain, your mind, and neuroscience for being so awesome!

So now, lets explore some of the findings from neuroscience that will enhance your work and make it highly effective.

Michael Graziano and Attention Schema Theory

When we talk about the neuroscience underpinning Deep Trance Identification we frequently refer to the work of Professor Michael Graziano of Princeton and his theory of Attention Schema Theory (AST).

AST explains that I interpret the actions and emotions of those around me by building an internal model, called an avatar, of each person I meet within my own mind. Now, of course, if I know that person well, over time I build a very detailed model of that person. Using this avatar, I can accurately predict his behavior and emotions in any given situation. If I don't know him well, I build a less detailed model. His avatar is less accurate, and I cannot predict his behavior.

For example: I have a very detailed model of my spouse but perhaps a very rough model of the barista at Starbucks who serves my coffee. Consider someone you know well; you probably have a detailed model of that person that would allow you to predict how she would react in any given situation. Now consider someone you have met but do not know well; you probably couldn't predict how that person would react in the same situation.

This is fairly uncontroversial; it is where Professor Graziano takes this theory next that is more interesting. He states that *you* also build an avatar of yourself and use this avatar to predict what will happen to you in any given situation.

For example: If I want to speak to a stranger at a party, I first imagine my avatar going to speak to the stranger and notice what happens. If it goes well for my avatar, then I will actually go and speak to the person in reality. But if it doesn't go so well for my avatar, I may have an attack of shyness.

Let's apply these principles to the Council of Inner Advisers. AST suggests that for each council member, my mind builds an avatar based on the information I know about him. The more I know about the person, the more accurate the avatar is; the less information I have, the more gaps I have to fill in. That's why is a great idea to learn as much as you can about each member of your council.

Now remember what the imaginary Thomas Edison told Napoleon Hill about hidden intelligences, or units, that exist disembodied from any physical person. Using AST, we can define these intelligences as avatars of archetypal persons, exactly the sort of person you would choose for your council and, therefore, exactly the sort of avatar your mind will create based on this archetype.

Are all these archetypes the same? Obviously not; you and I may both choose, say, Steve Jobs to be on our council. But my unconscious mind will always build a slightly different avatar of Jobs than your unconscious mind will.

In any case, it is not you that interacts with these archetypal avatars, according to Professor Graziano; it is your avatar of you that interacts with the archetypal avatars of your council members. And by interacting, your avatar of yourself is changed. It literally learns changes and evolves from interacting with these masters.

Mirror Neurons

Have you ever smiled at a baby and watched as she instantly smiled back? Or maybe you have heard someone laughing and began to laugh or giggle yourself even though you were not even sure why you laughed. Or perhaps you have noticed that when you and your partner are out at a romantic restaurant, you tend to pick up your glass of wine at almost the same time as each other? Well, neuroscience can explain all this! But before I get into the nuts and bolts of this, let me tell you a story about some monkeys in the Italian city of Parma.

Back in the 1990s, a group of researchers in Parma University (Di Pellegrino, Fadiga, Fogassi, Gallese, & Rizzolatt, *Experimental Brain Research* 1992) was studying the behavior of monkeys. In particular, they were tracking the brain activity when the monkeys made certain movements. The researchers were using brain-scanning technology to record their findings.

One day they inadvertently left the machines running while they were having a break. One of the researchers picked up a piece of fruit to snack on and as he did so, he realized that the recording of the brain activity of the monkeys was the same as if the monkeys themselves had picked up the piece of fruit. The brain cells of the monkeys associated with movement appeared to be activated *both* when they picked up the fruit *and* when they simply observed the researcher picking up the fruit.

Initially, the researchers were somewhat baffled by this apparent mirroring effect. But they didn't simply dismiss it as a fluke or coincidence; instead, they became curious about the effect and were keen to investigate it further. In doing so, they discovered what are now known as *mirror neurons*. They found that all the monkeys' brains responded in the same way whether they simply watched someone else pick up a piece of fruit or actually picked up the fruit themselves.

Fast-forward to the present day. You may have read that the concept of mirror neurons is something of a hot topic. Thus far, the existence of mirror neurons has been proven only in monkeys and not in the human brain. However, if you take a moment to consider this, it is nigh on impossible to detect these in the human brain without inserting some kind of probing device into the brain and measuring the result. This would be an unethical process to undertake on a live human (and I am certain there is an argument for it also being unethical to do so to our monkey relatives), so their existence in the human brain has been questioned. On the opposite side, some neuroscientists have gone to the other extreme and have stated that mirror neurons are responsible for human civilization. Only time will prove or disprove this theory—many believe this to be stretching the boundaries somewhat.

We have all experienced the mirror neuron effect in some way or the other during our lifetime. Did you answer yes or smile in recognition to at least one of the questions I asked at the beginning of this section? Have you ever noticed someone smiling at you and find that you were suddenly smiling back? Or maybe you've seen someone stub his toe and wince in pain alongside him? It appears that mirror neurons are designed for us to understand other people's behavior and emotions.

It was once thought that we use only a fraction of the brain—some people have suggested around 5 percent. Neuroscience research is suggesting that this is entirely untrue; in fact, our whole brain is active all the time. Neurons are firing continuously, seeking to connect with other neurons and fire as neural networks that we then call thoughts. We have many thoughts that lay below our conscious awareness, and some thoughts come into our conscious awareness.

By utilizing the CIA, you are adding additional neurological networks to your understanding of certain attributes. Let's say you have a member on your council who represents the ability to strategize, maybe it is Garry Kasparov the chess grand master, or Sun Tzu who wrote *The Art of War*. Whoever it is represents the ability to strategize. When connecting with this member, you will be activating your neurological networks associated with strategizing, enhancing this by adding in the representation of your specific council member and his abilities, and firing off your mirror neurons in the process. The larger the network, the more energy used by activation, the more likely you will be able to access these traits and abilities and bring these thoughts into conscious awareness.

Hebb's Law

There are more than a hundred billion neurons in the brain. Each neuron has a small cell-like body and a long projection-like tail that branches out from the main body. It is these branches that allow information to pass from one neuron to another. When information is passed from one to another, we call this electrical exchange *firing*. Each single neuron can be linked to tens of thousands of other neurons, and the more frequently these neurons pass information from one to another, the stronger the bond between them becomes.

You may be familiar with the phrase "Neurons that fire together, wire together." The scientist Donald Hebb coined this phrase back in the 1940s to describe how neurons link together to form stronger bonds of association. He wrote:

> Any two cells or systems of cells that are repeatedly active at the same time will tend to become "associated," so that activity in one facilitates activity in the other. (Hebb 1949)

Neuroscience is still a burgeoning area of knowledge, and there is still much to be discovered. However, most neuroscientists agree about how neurons fire and wire together. And they agree to such an extent that they call it a law. When two neurons are fired at the same time, they become sensitive to each other, eventually wiring together.

Hebb's Law: Neurons that fire together wire together.

The more frequently two neurons or neurological networks fire simultaneously, the stronger a bond or connection is created between them. Let's put this in a context that might be familiar to most people: Imagine you go to an event and meet some great people. Maybe you sit next to one particular person with whom you have a brief and pleasant social interaction. Sometime later you meet that person again at another social event. You may say something like, "Oh, hello. Didn't we meet at XYZ event? How have you been?" This time your interaction is longer, and maybe you have a few more moments to talk with each other, or perhaps find something that you both have in common. You meet for a third or fourth time and gradually a deeper friendship forms. Perhaps you decide to go for coffee or a drink. Before long, you have become the very best of friends—you have created a strong link between the two of you. It is the same process for neurons that fire together in the brain. You can see Hebb's law in action, and just as the example of establishing a friendship takes some time, so does the process of creating a strong neurological pathway between two separate neurological networks.

Lets put this in the context of the CIA Pattern. Through this pattern, we hope to gain insight and understanding, enhance certain skills, and receive guidance. Meeting frequently with your council ensures that you are strengthening your bond with your advisers. Every time you meet you grow closer and gain deeper insight and connection with these figures. On a neurological level, you are stimulating the various neurological networks that represent the specific traits within your brain. The more frequently you do this, the stronger the neurological networks are linked and the council members' attributes and traits will be more readily available to you.

Visualization

The concept that the brain doesn't differentiate between what is seen and what is strongly imagined has long been a tenet of hypnosis. However, it is only in recent years that neuroscientists have been able to give us a scientific explanation of what happens in the brain for this to be so.

Around the turn of the millennium Gabriel Kreiman, Christof Koch, and Itzhak Fried (Krieman 2000) from UCLA and Caltech were studying areas of the brain responsible for certain electrical activity—particularly the hippocampus, which is responsible for the formation of long-term memories—in patients with a specific form of epilepsy known as intractable epilepsy. As part of this study, patients were asked to look at everyday objects, such as a baseball, an emotional face, or food. The neurons responsible for encoding this information fired off and were recorded by the scientists. The patients were then asked to recall or bring to their mind's eye these same objects. In the majority of cases, the scientists found that the same neurons were activated when recalling or imagining the objects. This remarkable study demonstrates that the coding of objects within the brain is likely the same whether the object is seen in real life, imagined, or recalled.

This is hugely important in the CIA Pattern, as the internal representations you create will fire off the same neural networks as if you were seeing and interacting with these folks in real life!

Working Memory

Your working memory is constantly active and acts as a "control panel" for everything you do and everything you feel. Working memory is comprised of three parts:

1. A movie screen
2. A soundtrack
3. A title

Whether you are aware of it or not, you are making images and pictures inside your mind constantly.

These images and pictures projected onto this movie screen of your mind could be memories, a future plan, or simply a daydream.

Along with the movie is a soundtrack. For example: If you were to imagine an ice cream truck coming down the street on a hot summer's day, it's quite possible that your brain has provided the tinkling bell or tinny song of the ice cream truck. This represents the soundtrack appropriate for the specific movie.

The last aspect of working memory is often considered the most important. This is the meaning you make of the movie; we call this the title. If you think about the ice cream truck coming down the street on a hot summer's day and hearing the tinny song heralding its arrival, what meaning might you make of this? Maybe your title would be something like, "Yum" or "That Day Was Fantastic."

The interesting thing, however, is that even though we may make wonderful pictures in our mind, both consciously and unconsciously, with fantastic soundtracks, sometime the title we associate with these two aspects may not be positive. As this is the meaning we place on the experience, it can have a profound effect on our interpretation of it. Let's take our previous example and say that in your mind, an ice cream truck is coming down the street and the tinny song is playing. The meaning you put on this is "I used to have fun." Even writing that sentence makes me feel a little sad. Perhaps you have had a similar experience. If so, take a moment to change the title of this movie into something more positive for yourself and notice how it is different now.

Of course, there is much more to it than simply making a picture, adding a soundtrack, and creating a positive title. No doubt, we have all had some experience where we have run pictures in our minds of an upcoming event and have added a positive title, yet when the event occurred, it didn't turn out the way we had envisioned it. Why did this happen? This is likely because the movie we were playing in our mind didn't have the appropriate title.

Researchers at the University of California ran an interesting study using positive thoughts and visualizations. They asked students to make positive images of themselves taking tests. They asked one group to imagine that they've scored well in an exam and to add a positive title. Interestingly enough, instead of helping the students to improve their grades, this process proved counterproductive. Overall, the students' grades in this group went down because they had spent less time studying. The issue with the visualization was that the title that the researchers had suggested to the students was one that did not inspire them to work or study because it presumed that they had already put in the work and would simply achieve a high grade without studying. The title was something like "I will get a high mark in this exam." This title decreased motivation to study in the students, and they scored a lower mark. A second group was asked to visualize themselves studying, working hard, and preparing for the examination. Interestingly enough, this group scored higher marks in the real-life examination.

As the CIA Pattern is essentially a visualization, it relies on working memory to ensure its success. By visiting your council, asking for guidance, interviewing individual members, listening to suggestions, and having private meetings, you are giving yourself many reference experiences from the lives of your council members. Therefore, it is vitally important to visualize as clearly as possible, to add a soundtrack to these visualizations, and to include a positive title for each interaction with your Council of Advisers.

The people you select to be on your council are likely to be people who are known to you either personally or as historical or well-known figures. You have chosen them because you admire something about them or recognize a certain trait that would be useful to you. You have to know something about each person to have selected her. Your mirror neurons will already be activated through these external experiences with these people. You may have interacted with them in real life or via films, books, TV, or other media. The manner in which you interacted with them is less important than the fact that some kind of interaction has happened. Remember, when the monkeys saw the researcher lift a piece of fruit it was as though they were lifting a piece of fruit themselves. So each time you've seen an actor on screen, on the stage, or come to life in your own imagination through reading about her, your mirror neurons had activated and you were already establishing reference experiences. When your council members appear in your visualizations of your CIA, the neural networks associated with each individual will be activated and new neural networks and pathways created as you interact with them in trance.

Dopamine

Dopamine is a neurotransmitter that plays an important role in helping us to learn. Dopamine stabilizes our working memory; it helps to keep the right movies playing on our internal movie screen with the correct soundtrack and with the appropriate title. The second function of dopamine is that it instructs the hippocampus—the part of the brain where long-term memories are laid down—to be aware that whatever the brain is experiencing in any given moment is important and needs to be paid attention to. This is the starting point of creating a longer, more substantial memory. So dopamine is a very important neurotransmitter within our brain.

There are a two main ways to help create dopamine. Both are simple, easy, and fun. The first one is to sort for things that are new and different. This means that it is a great idea to take some time each day to look for novelty, to train yourself to become more aware of the changes and differences in your environment, and to search for new things.

The second way to create dopamine is a really fun way. And that's it! It is simply to have fun. Find things that you enjoy doing. Go to movies that make you laugh. Sing in the shower. Collect stamps. Play sports. Watch your favorite TV shows. And enjoy life! Simply by smiling you create dopamine in your brain and enhance your learning and your ability to form long-term memories. And the amazing thing is that you can easily help others to enhance their dopamine production too. Remember how our mirror neurons work? When you smile at someone, that person usually smiles back Well, by doing so, you help that person to create dopamine in his brain. So go out and influence someone else's brain by smiling at them, ensure you take plenty of dopamine "time outs," and have fun!

The CIA Pattern in of itself is a fun experience, and I highly suggest including one member of your council to represent fun.

Ideomotor Responses

Did you know that all our physical actions and movements are under our unconscious control? You may think that you make specific decisions to move in a certain way, to pick up your phone, to take a drink, to scratch your nose. However, we know that the programs for movement, gestures, motions, and all physical actions are controlled by the unconscious mind. (Benjamin Libet has published extensively on this subject.)

We also know that the entire brain is continually active forming recognized thought. And this is true of the neurons, networks, and circuits in the motor cortex too. As a result, we are continually making movements. We gesture when talking without thinking about how or when to move our hands. Our faces make tiny movements, or microexpressions, that can reveal our emotions. Our body moves in almost imperceptible ways much of the time. These unconscious movements can be used to disclose unconscious responses through a process called *ideomotor signals*.

Ideomotor signals are simply small movements, for example, finger twitches, mouth or facial movements, or tiny head nods. We associate these tiny movements with certain states, including those of agreement and disagreement. The head nod is widely accepted as a gesture for agreement in Western cultures. Although it is often used with more conscious awareness, a tiny head nod can be seen as an unconscious sign of agreement. Indeed, the nod doesn't even need to be that "micro." Look around at any audience, say, at a lecture, meeting, workshop, or play. Notice how many blatant head nods happen that the head nodder is probably totally unaware of!

Ideomotor signals can be actively set up with a client or with yourself to communicate with the unconscious mind. (We use them later in this book.)

Physical/Body Microgestures

Close your eyes and ask your unconscious mind to show you a "yes." Be open for anything to be the "yes" signal. You may experience a finger twitch, a word, or internal sound. Some people notice a sensation in the body or see a color in their mind's eye. Simply be still and wait for something to occur.

Once you have received a "yes," thank your unconscious mind. Now ask for a "no" signal. It is often useful to spell out the word *n-o* so as not to confuse it with the word *know*. Once again, wait for something to happen and be open to receiving any signal. Once you have it, thank the unconscious mind. Now repeat the exercise with the "maybe" signal.

Using a Pendulum

Hold the pendulum lightly between your thumb and forefinger, and ask your unconscious mind to show you a "yes." The pendulum will begin to swing in a certain direction, maybe right to left, front and back, or maybe in a circle either clockwise or counterclockwise. Note that if the pendulum remains completely still, this may be the signal itself. Thank the unconscious mind, and repeat the exercise for both the "no" signal and the "maybe" signal.

Chapter 4: Inside the CIA Toolbox

Before we move into the details of how the CIA Pattern works, we need to outline the necessary skills and techniques utilized in this pattern:

- Visualization
- Trance or hypnosis
- Self-hypnosis
- Association and dissociation

Visualization

In a moment, I am going to ask you to close your eyes and imagine seeing someone you really like. This may be a good friend, partner, parent, child, or even your favorite pet. Go ahead now and close your eyes and bring this person or pet to mind for a few moments.

How was that? You may have found this particularly easy. You may have found that you were already bringing that person to mind, possibly having a few different options run through your mind when you were reading the directions. Our mind takes in, sorts, and classifies information via all five senses, and we store vast amounts of information visually.

Despite our storing and accessing information visually, some people may find it more difficult to visualize than others. If this is the case for you, then we suggest a little more practice. The truth is that everyone visualizes. The visual sense is known to be superfast, and we make visual images all the time. Sometimes, however, these pictures are so fast that they whizz through the unconscious mind with very little conscious awareness. It is easy to strengthen this visual "muscle"; it simply takes a time and practice. One way to do this is to visually recall very familiar places or people. You may wish to start by simply thinking about your front door.

As you think about your front door, what color is it? What is the handle like? Where is the lock? Is it on the left or the right? Do you have a number on your door? In your mind, you might look at the number. Now go into your house. Which room are you in first? Does your front door lead directly into your living space? Maybe it leads to a vestibule or hallway? When you look to your left, what do you see? Now look to your right, and see what you see? Walk into your living room. Where is your sofa? Where is the window? Are there blinds, shades, or curtains? If so, what color are they? Where is the light coming from?

You can continue this kind of exercise for as long as you wish. It is useful to do this type of exercise a few times a day to train your visual muscle so that it becomes very used to seeing things in your mind's eye. Some people are able to visualize very strongly. The images they see in their mind's eye are similar to how they experience the real world. Other people will have a more hazy or fuzzy representation when they visualize. Either way works beautifully.

Hypnosis or Trance

We use the words *hypnosis* and *trance* interchangeably throughout this book. We understand that you may already be a certified hypnotist, familiar with working with clients and taking people into trance. We are also aware that you may not be a certified hypnotist, and have less experience and understanding of what trance is and how to access it. If you are familiar with hypnosis, you may wish to skip ahead while we have a brief discussion about trance and the unconscious mind.

I'm sure you are aware that we all have a conscious mind and an unconscious mind. The conscious mind likes to think that it is in control of everything; however, it is really the unconscious mind that is in control. The unconscious mind controls the heart rate, digestion, hair growth, and all of our body functions. We do not have to consciously think about these things—they just happen. The unconscious mind is the place of creativity, where good ideas and "aha" moment spring from. It is also the place where some people generate issues or problems. Think about it. I expect that at some point in your life, you have had an issue or a problem but that you didn't simply wake up one day and decide consciously to have—it just seemed to happen. Now, you may be able to consciously figure out why the problem started, or what even triggered the problem in you. Nevertheless, it still probably felt as though it was beyond your conscious control. That is because it was generated in the unconscious mind.

Fortunately, the unconscious mind is also the place of all of our resources. This is why it is the best place to go to when solving any issues or problems. (By the way, if you still have that problem and want to change, then you may wish to consider seeing a certified hypnotist.)

Let me ask you another question. Do you dream at night? If so, it is likely that you dream in pictures. This is another example of how the unconscious mind works. The unconscious mind is communicating to us, learning new things, putting ideas together, consolidating and practicing skills whilst we dream. The unconscious mind speaks to us and communicates in pictures and symbols and images, whereas the conscious mind communicates through words. The conscious mind likes logic and order, as opposed to the unconscious mind that is the vast array of pure potentiality and creativity.

Of course, these two minds work together all the time, and information or thoughts move from the unconscious mind into our conscious awareness. It is as though there is a doorway between these two minds and the doorway is usually open to only small amounts of information brought to our conscious awareness. Using hypnosis, we are able to open this doorway more fully so that the vast resources of the unconscious mind can be utilized. Opening this doorway can be thought of as entering hypnosis.

We believe that trance, or hypnosis, is a frequently occurring and completely natural phenomenon and that we open this doorway to the unconscious mind numerous times every day. If you have ever watched a fantastic movie and felt caught up in the story line, or read a novel that you felt deeply involved in and could see the characters and places in your mind's eye, or maybe daydreamed about an event coming up in the future, then you have experienced a moment of trance, or hypnosis. You have been doing this all your life! Every time you have daydreamed or thought about a future event, you have been in trance. If you have ever been so engrossed in something that you didn't hear your name called, you have been in trance. If you have ever missed your exit or turn while driving because your mind was elsewhere, you have been in trance. Of course, these examples are of naturally occurring trances. We can also deliberately take ourselves into trance too by using self-hypnosis.

The CIA Pattern is a process that can be used both in a client/hypnotist situation and individually for personal change. If you intend to use this pattern for personal change, we suggest that you become familiar with taking yourself into self-hypnosis.

Self-Hypnosis

Self-hypnosis is a wonderful skill to have, but it does take some practice to build the technique so that you can access this state easily and whenever you wish to. In our experience, it is really very easy. It is it can be as simple as closing your eyes and imagining.

Here is one method for going into self-hypnosis:

- Begin by finding a comfortable place where you will not be disturbed during this trance. Take a moment to get comfortable and find something in front of you to gaze at. We suggest this be at least 3 feet away. Allow your vision to narrow down to the tiniest detail, and focus on that point. You can notice any differences in color, variations in light and shadow, even the texture of that point. Imagine you could narrow your gaze down even more so that it's almost as if you could see the atoms and molecules that make up that point.

- Next, allow your gaze to relax and your focus to soften. Still looking at that point, let your vision expand so you can take in more of the space in front of you. The more you relax your eyes as you keep looking at that point, the more you can take in everything that is to your sides, above you, and below you. You could allow your awareness to expand, and as your vision expands, you can sense the distance between yourself and the walls in front of you, behind you, and to your sides. You could be aware even of the space from the top of your head to the ceiling.

- As you do this, notice the comfortable, relaxing feeling deepening in your body and mind. Allow it to spread from the top of your head to the tips of your toes. It is as if each time you exhale, another wave of peace, comfort, and relaxation passes through you. When you are ready, you can close your eyes and relax even more deeply, enjoying the comfort in your body and the quietness in your mind.

This is one simple method for going into self-hypnosis. We are aware that there are many other options. Find one that you like, and become familiar with the process.

Association and Dissociation

In simple terms, association is visualizing an event—past, future, or imaginary—and you are experiencing this event as though you were living it in the present moment.

Dissociation is the opposite of this. Dissociation is recalling or imagining an event—past, future, or imaginary—and you are watching it as an observer, as though you can see it on a movie screen or playing out in the space around you, but you are observing yourself going through the different motions in the event.

Association = being fully in the event

Dissociation = being an observer to the event, watching yourself going through the event

Both of these are important skills when using the CIA Pattern, and you will need to use them either with your client or yourself as you go through the steps of this pattern.

It is highly likely that when leading yourself through this pattern using self-hypnosis that you will become associated into your own experience. The experience will be self-directed, and you will be fully *in* the experience seeing it through your own eyes, hearing it through your own ears, and interacting with your council members within the space that you create. You will likely be sensing and experiencing the feelings and emotions in real time.

Guiding a Client into an Associated Experience

If you are leading a client through the CIA Pattern, some linguistic shifts are necessary to help your client more easily associate into and dissociate from her personal experience. The key linguistic change you will need to make when associating someone is to move into using present tense language.

For example: Let's say your client is already in trance and you want to take him to a moment when he is interacting with the council. Maybe they have a specific question or dilemma they wish to address or resolve.

Here is a client transcript highlighting the linguistic shifts to help him associate. (You will have already taken your client into a light trance).

> Coach: In a moment, you are going to your meeting space. I know you have been there before. Do you remember what it was like?
>
> Client: Yes. It was in a suburban house, and we were sitting around the kitchen table.
>
> Coach: That's right; you were sitting around the kitchen table. Do you remember anything else about the kitchen?
>
> Client: Yes. It looked like it was from the 1970s.
>
> Coach: How wonderful! The 1970s! And what are you *seeing* now?
>
> Client: The tabletop is a blue Formica, and the chairs are red.
>
> Coach: Yes. What else are you *seeing* now?

Client: There is a window to my left.

Coach: What are you *hearing* now?

Client: Not much. There is a slight sound of traffic somewhere outside, but it is pretty quiet and restful.

Coach: That's right. There *is* a slight sound of traffic somewhere outside but it *is* pretty quiet and restful. Now, I want you to *begin to see* your council members entering the room.

(The session would continue from here with the council meeting.)

The key thing to notice here is that the coach helped the client to record a previous experience of the space and shifted into the present tense, helping the client to fully associate into the moment ready for the upcoming experience.

Guiding a Client into a Dissociated Experience

Dissociation is the opposite of association. There may be times when it is useful for the client or you to step out of your own body and watch the event play out, as though you were a fly on the wall observing what is happening. This is often called being in *third position* and gives a different perspective. From this position, you can be more objective, as you will not be experiencing the emotions involved in the event. In my experience, we tend to use dissociation less in the CIA Pattern, although it is an important skill to have and can be used powerfully and effectively, particularly if an objective view is needed.

Here is another example of the same client in his 1970s kitchen with his council and the coach using a dissociative moment.

Coach: So what's happening now?

Client: Sophocles has been holding the floor for ages and doesn't seem to want to let anyone else participate in this discussion. (Smiling) He sure has a lot to say!

Coach: What is happening with the other council members?

Client: I'm not sure; I'm so entranced by Sophocles.

Coach: Is he saying something of great importance that is valuable to you? Are you getting a lesson here?

Client: I'm not entirely sure.

Coach: OK. What I'd like you to do for a moment is to imagine that you can step outside of your own body and stand aside from the kitchen table. Maybe you are like the fly on the wall, or you're simply standing in the doorway watching and observing what is happening. Let me know when you have done that.

Client: Yes.

Coach: Great. Can you see your council members?

Client: Yes.

Coach: Do you see that "you" is also sitting at the table?
Do you see Brian there?

Client: Yes, I see him.

Coach: Great. And from this position of neutrality, what do you notice?

Client: I can see the other members are listening and nodding in agreement, but they're fidgety, so maybe it's time for Brian to thank Sophocles and move the meeting forward.

Coach: Great. And now I would like you to float back in to yourself fully and completely and do that. Thank Sophocles and move the meeting forward.

(Client floats back into himself and the meeting can continue from here.)

You will note that the coach asked the client to step outside of himself and to take a fly-on-the-wall, or observer, position. To maintain this dissociated position, the coach refers to that "you over there" or "Brian." This dissociative language helps to keep the client from stepping back into himself.

A Slightly Different Approach Is Needed when Using Self-Hypnosis

Because there is no external hypnotist or coach to guide the interaction and self-hypnosis is so very associative, it is more challenging to dissociate when doing self-hypnosis. I (Sarah) have found that if I wish to view an interaction from a more dissociated position, I have to enter self-hypnosis with the intention of viewing the experience from the fly-on-the-wall position.

For example: If I wanted to visit my council to observe how we all interact and work together as a group, I would set my intention of doing this before going into self-hypnosis. Once inside self-hypnosis, I can visit my council as though looking through the window or standing in the corner or simply being an invisible observer of Sarah and her council members interacting. This can give me valuable insights as to how well we are working as a team.

Chapter 5: Creating Your Council

As we have previously mentioned, you can create numerous councils. However, one thing is certain: for each council you establish, you have to select members to become part of that council. There are two basic ways of selecting a council member, and we outline them within this chapter. There are also a number of additional aspects to consider when creating your council, such as how many members there should be, when and how members leave or join the council, and how to create a balanced, diverse council. We address all these areas in this chapter.

Whether you are creating a general council or establishing a council for a specific purpose, there are two basic methods of creating your group. I have used both methods at different times—and both methods works perfectly well.

In brief, you can select either the people you would like to have or the attribute you desire. Inevitably, it becomes a mix of both, so the order in which you do this becomes less important.

Method 1: People First

Make a list of people you admire, people who you believe you can learn from, people who you think could offer good advice or constructive criticism. These people can be well known or obscure, famous or infamous, alive or dead, friends or family members; people from history, from fiction, or even from mythology. We suggest that you make as long a list as possible at first. Consider popular or famous people who are living now, those who have passed on, those in your family, friends, or colleagues What books, plays, or movies do you love? And which characters stick out in your mind? Think about all aspects of you life and where you live, where you work, your hobbies and interests, and make a list of the people who you admire in these areas. This should provide a long list from which you will be able to make your selections.

Method 2: Attribute First

This is often the method I choose if I am creating a council to serve for a very specific purpose, although it will work perfectly well for creating a general council too. I explain both here.

Creating a Council for a Specific Purpose

Take a few moments to sit quietly and consider the purpose of your council. Maybe you want a council to give you guidance in your career or your relationships. I (Sarah) created a specific council to guide and assist in the writing of this book. (See Appendix 1 for more details.)

As you consider your specific purpose, make a list of the attributes you already have and aspects you are good at. Now make a list of your weak points, the attributes that you feel you are lacking, or areas where you know you could use guidance. This is a time to be very honest with yourself and allow yourself to recognize your shortcomings.

When making this list, the attributes you write down don't necessarily have to fit into a defined or specific emotion or skill. For example: When creating my council for writing this book, I knew from past experiences with writing that I could get lazy and procrastinate, so one of the attributes I wanted was an active "just-do-it-ness." I could have selected the word *motivator*, but that didn't seem to have enough energy behind it for me. So the phrase *just-do-it-ness* was the one I wrote down on my list and was one of the characteristics that I eventually selected for my council.

Once you have a list of attributes, select the top five or six and, taking them one at a time, consider which person embodies this specific trait. You may come up with a few options for each attribute, and from here, you can select the one person who you think would be the best adviser. Remember, you can pick from a very wide range of people—well known, fictional, friends, superheroes, coworkers, family members.

One important point to note here is that each of us (including fictional characters) has a breadth of emotions and negative attributes, along with positive ones. Steve Jobs is a member of my council for his creative flair and his ability to think outside of the box. But I am well aware that in his own life he struggled with personal relationships, and that is an area that I would not be seeking guidance from him!

Remember, you are selecting members for one specific aspect of their personality, and when you meet your council members, you will explain the reason you have selected them and outline your expectations from them. You will go through each attribute one by one, allowing yourself to find people who embody this aspect and selecting the best person to invite onto your council.

Hill himself in his book *Think and Grow Rich* offered us some fine examples of conversations with his council members where he clearly lays out the reasons each person was selected. For example:

Mr. Edison, ... I wish to acquire from you the marvelous spirit of faith, with which you have uncovered so many of Nature's secrets, the spirit of unremitting toil with which you have so often wrested victory from defeat. (Hill 1937)

The following is an excerpt from my journal documenting my experience of creating a CIA for writing this book.

I began by making a list of attributes that I would find most beneficial. I sat quietly for a moment and allowed my breathing to regulate, closed my eyes, and took myself into a light trance. I asked my unconscious mind to generate the qualities and attributes that would be most beneficial to me in writing this book. After a few moments, numerous words appeared in my mind, and I brought myself out of trance and wrote them down. My list included creativity, just-do-it-ness, being in flow, perseverance, timekeeping, prioritizing, fun, getting things done, experience.

Looking at this list, one particular attribute stood out to me, and that was the quality of "experience." I have written a few books in the past, so I knew I had some experience, and yet this word had popped into my mind. I just sat with this word for a few moments, contemplating it and wondering why or how I could use this aspect. In just a few moments, I came to the realization that I was looking for the experience of somebody who is a professional writer, someone who has devoted his or her life to writing, someone who is famous for being a writer. My jobs have included being a teacher, hypnotist, change-worker, yet writing was something that I had never expected to do. As soon as I began to think about someone who is a writer, someone who's written many books, the author Stephen King came to mind. This was very interesting because I have never read any Stephen King novels! I did, however, know that he is a prolific writer, has published many books, and is widely known and admired. I immediately wrote his name down on my list of potential council members.

From there, I went back to my list of attributes and began to tease out the top five or six qualities that I thought would be the most useful for me. My final list was creativity, just-do-it-ness, sense of humor, experience, productivity, focus. Taking each of these qualities one at a time, I invited my unconscious mind to generate an individual who embodied each particular trait. This part of the process, for me, was relatively fast. Within a few moments, I already had a suggestion for four of the qualities. I have selected Stephen King for experience, Albert Einstein for creativity, Steve Jobs for focus, and Shawn Carson (my husband and coauthor of this book) for productivity.

(The other two places were filled later. You can read about the process in later in this chapter. For a full account, see Appendix 1.)

Creating an Archetypes Council

An archetypes council is made up of people who embody archetypes. For example, you may wish to include a teacher, warrior, hero, creative visionary, explorer, caregiver. Your General Council is likely to be made up of archetypes.

Take some time to consider which archetypes you would like to have on your council. Once you have selected six or so, take each archetype individually and allow yourself to come up with a list of people who personify this specific trait.

For example: You may wish to have a caregiver archetype, and you may come up with Mother Theresa, Oskar Schindler, Maria from the *Sound of Music* movie, your mother/grandmother, and your friend who rescues dogs. From this list, select the one who you believe embodies this trait the most and who would be a great council member. Remember, when selecting your council members, you will want to have a range of archetypes, balance and diversity, and people who exhibit traits that you are lacking or need more of.

Conscious and Unconscious Selection of Members

Your Council of Inner Advisers is part of your unconscious reality; therefore, selecting members for your council solely by a conscious process is unlikely to have the profound effect you desire. This being the case, we strongly advise that you include your unconscious mind in the selection of members for your council. This can be done in a number of ways.

Whether you select possible members by person first or attribute first, it is likely that at some point you will have a list of potential candidates for the positions you would like to fill. Once you have a list, you can do a number of processes to unconsciously select the right member. Here are a few possibilities.

Ideomotor Signals

Set up ideomotor "yes," "no," and "maybe" signals for yourself. You can do this simply by closing your eyes and asking your unconscious mind to show you a "yes" and waiting for something to occur. Oftentimes people feel a finger twitch or maybe a sensation in the body or a color or hear a word or sound. Be still and wait for something to occur. Be open to it being anything. Once you have received a "yes," thank your unconscious mind and ask for a "no" signal. It is often useful to spell out the word *n-o* so as not to confuse it with *know*. Once again, wait for something to happen and be open to receiving any signal. Once you have it, thank your unconscious mind and repeat with the "maybe" signal. Once you have all three ideomotor signals in place, simply bring to mind each candidate and wait for the unconscious response.

Pendulum

Similar to the above, but this time you can use a pendulum. Hold the pendulum lightly between your thumb and forefinger and ask your unconscious mind to show you a "yes." The pendulum will begin to swing in a certain direction, laterally (right/ left), front and back, or maybe in a circle clockwise or counterclockwise. Note that if the pendulum remains completely still, this may be the signal itself. Thank your unconscious mind, and repeat the process for both the "no" and the "maybe" signals. Again, once you have the directions clearly defined, bring to mind each candidate in turn and ask if this person is the right member for the place on your council. Observe the movement of the pendulum in your selection, and don't be surprised if your unconscious surprises you with its choices!

Hypnotic Interview

Find a quiet comfortable place to sit and close your eyes. Allow yourself to relax, and set your mind to considering your council. Think about why you are creating this particular council and what your goal and desired outcome are. Now bring to mind either the attribute/position you are wishing to fill (for example, the warrior position on your archetypes council), and reflect on each candidate one by one. You can simply picture them in your mind's eye and just get a sense of who is right, or you can spend a few moments interviewing them for the position. Usually just bringing them to mind individually is enough for your unconscious mind to make the choice.

Here is an example of using unconscious selection of a member, the pendulum, and the hypnotic interview from my experience of creating a CIA for this book. I was looking for women to fill the roles of just-do-it-ness and fun.

> Whilst in bed and just before falling asleep, I took myself to my usual relaxation place, a beautiful white marble pavilion, and simply asked my unconscious mind to come up with a few possibilities of women who could fulfill these particular roles. Before I knew it, I had fallen asleep, and whilst I was sleeping, my unconscious mind was working hard. I have an awareness of waking lightly a few times during the night, and each time I was thinking about a woman who would be great for one of these roles. When I fully woke the next morning, I had five women who were potential candidates for the role of motivator and one woman, the British comedienne Victoria Wood, to fulfill the role of fun.

> I decided to ask my unconscious mind, using my pendulum, to show me which of the five women would be the best fit. I sat quietly holding my pendulum between my thumb and pointer finger. I asked the pendulum to show me a "yes" signal, a "no" signal, and a "maybe" signal. Once these directions had been established, I went through the list of women, one by one, asking my unconscious mind to show me via the pendulum whether they would be a "yes," a "no," or a "maybe."

Queen Elizabeth I was one of my choices, and as I asked whether she would be the right person to fulfill the role of motivator, the pendulum began to swing very clearly in the "no" direction. I thanked my unconscious mind and moved to my second test, Queen Elizabeth II. The pendulum stayed still in its "maybe" position. I thanked my unconscious mind again and moved to the third woman on the list. The next two candidates, Temple Grandin and the little girl from the Disney movie *Brave*, also received a "maybe" signal from my unconscious mind. The last candidate was Eleanor Roosevelt, and I received a strong "yes" signal from my unconscious mind.

At this point, I decided to also do a hypnotic interview with each candidate just to double-check. I closed my eyes and went inside and took myself to the white pavilion. Sitting on one of the comfortable white sofas, I invited Queen Elizabeth I to come into the pavilion. I stood, curtsied, and welcomed her to the space. I immediately felt that something was off. I realized that we were not equals, that she exuded such royal presence and expected to be so much higher than anybody else that she probably wasn't the best choice for position on the council where everyone is equal and everyone shares. I invited Queen Elizabeth I to sit with me, and for some unusual reason, my unconscious mind kept moving her over to my right and slightly out of my view. Whenever I changed positions so that we were sitting opposite each other, Elizabeth I continued to move to my right and out of my view. I took this at as a very strong indication that Queen Elizabeth I was indeed not the right person to fulfill this role on my council. I thanked her for her time and escorted her out of the white pavilion. I wondered whether part of the reason she was moving out of sight and over to my right was that I had asked her into my own unique personal space as opposed to meeting in either neutral space or a place that she was familiar with.

For my meeting with Queen Elizabeth II, I decide to trust my unconscious mind to select the right place for us to meet. The scene opened into a private office space that I assumed was an office space in Buckingham Palace. Queen Elizabeth II was seated behind an ornate desk in a beautifully appointed room. As I approached the desk, I curtsied and immediately began to explain why we were meeting, about the role and function that would be required of her. Queen Elizabeth II smiled a big smile and said, "Oh, you think I could do that?" It was such a funny moment to me because it seemed to show a vulnerability that I had not expected from the queen. I smiled and giggled slightly and said, "Of course you can do this. I would be honored to have you on my council. Is this something you'd be interested in doing?" Queen Elizabeth II smiled and said, "Well, thank you so very much for thinking of me. I would be delighted to help; however, I'm unusually busy at this time." I thanked her for her time and for her service and wished her a happy 90th birthday.

(This process continued with all the other potential candidates until both positions were filled.)

Of course, the entire selection process can be done unconsciously too. Simply decide upon the attribute you would like and allow yourself to go into self-hypnosis and see who shows up!

How Many Members?

The question of how many members you would like on your council is really up to you. Napoleon Hill initially had nine members, and this eventually expanded to more than 50! However, in my experience, I have found there to be a sweet spot in the five–seven range. Having too many people on the council means having to remember who is on the council; handling the meetings might be trickier too. Having between five and seven members means that council meetings tend to flow more smoothly and each person has time to offer advise and counsel. Remember, this is your council, and you can always add, expand, and replace members as you wish. You may also wish to create subcommittees for specific tasks. These can include members from your general committee as well as members co-opted to fulfill a specific role.

Permanent and Temporary Members

Your Council of Inner Advisers can include both permanent members and temporary members. Just as the United Nations Security Council has five permanent members and a number of members who rotate over a set period, you can set up something similar. You may wish to create your general CIA of five to seven permanent members and then, if you know you have a specific issue to address, co-opt additional members with a specific skill set, knowledge base, or experience for a time. Let's say you have a permanent CIA that consists of Nelson Mandela, Florence Nightingale, Coco Chanel, Wolverine, and your cousin Fred, and you wish to get advice on a relationship issue. You may wish to set up a completely new additional CIA to give advice on this area, or you may decide to add a few temporary members to your General Council, such as Paul Newman and

Joanne Woodward, Dr. Ruth, or even Lady from *Lady and the Tramp*!

Members Leaving or Joining the Council

Just as you can have temporary members and additional subcommittees, members can also leave or join the council. You may find that a particular member is not working out for you and you wish to replace that member, or that she expresses a desire to "retire." If either of these occur, simply take time to thank the adviser for her participation, inform her of why you no longer require her presence (if she is not working out for you), and ask her whether she would like to let the other council members know of her leaving or if you, as chairperson, should inform the council. Either way, it is important to have closure.

If a new member is joining the council, similarly there needs to be an introduction. The group dynamic of the council will alter if any changes are made. Therefore, it is important for a new member to be properly introduced to the group.

Balancing Your Council

Creating balance within your council is an important aspect to consider. You want to ensure that your council is made up of members who are not too much like yourself, who can bring an alternative point of view, different experiences, or thoughts opposed to yours. You will also want to consider your personal strengths and abilities AND your weaker points and shortcomings. If you are setting up a council for a specific goal, you may wish to ask yourself, "What skills or personal qualities will help me to achieve this goal? What ability or attributes could I really use here?" Once you have identified these, you may wish to specifically choose members who can balance you by providing strength, knowledge, and ability in these weaker areas.

You will want to take into account the age of the people you select—perhaps having people both older and younger than yourself is a good mix. Think about the gender combination on your council, and consider what the positives and negatives may be for having a council of all men, all women, or a mix of both. You may also want to include a mixture of historical, fictional, and real-life people on your council.

With all this in mind, it is important to realize that this process is ultimately an unconscious one, and you will probably find that some of the people you select consciously simply don't work out. Bringing you unconscious mind into the selection process will offer up many new and different people, some of whom you may never have considered if you were to just think of a person consciously to invite to the council. My council for writing this book consists of four men and three women. They are all older than I am, and it works beautifully!

Considering having a balanced council is important, but bear in mind that it doesn't always work out that way!

Chapter 6: Creating the Council Chamber

For every council you create, you will also have to establish the place where you will meet. We have all had experiences of attending meetings at work or at home, personal or professional, and every one of these meetings has taken place in a particular space. The space these meetings take place in may be a real physical space, or nowadays with the technology we have available to us, our meetings may be virtual and take place somewhere on the ether of the interwebs.

For your Council of Inner Advisers, you will want to establish a meeting space, and aleph point, a "home" for you and your council members to meet. If you are accustomed to doing any self-hypnosis or meditation practice, you may already have a safe place, a comfortable retreat, a place in nature that you go to relax. This can be a fantastic starting point for your unconscious mind to create your special meeting place.

Your special meeting place does not have to be a magnificent castle or sumptuous palace; it simply has to be a place where you are supremely comfortable and totally at ease. A place where you know you can easily discuss anything, be frank with your council members, and be open to the suggestions and guidance they offer. It can be a simple cabin in the woods, a kitchen table, a picnic blanket in a meadow, a modern corporate boardroom, a campfire under the stars, or anything else that your unconscious mind brings forth. As you are well aware by now, the CIA process is a highly hypnotic process, one that utilizes the power of the unconscious mind. We highly suggest that you allow your unconscious mind to create the meeting place for you.

This is very easy to do. You can think about this process in five easy steps:

1. Enter trance.
2. Find the place of comfort.
3. Orient to the location.
4. Find a structure, building, or functional space.
5. Find the meeting room or space.

We'll go through each of these points in turn.

Enter Trance

Remember, this does not need to be a particularly deep trance. In fact, if you are working with a client, it is often beneficial for your client to be able to speak so you can help him track his experience. If you are using self-hypnosis, then a light trance may also be beneficial, as you may wish to move out of trance occasionally to write notes about your experience and then take yourself back into trance for the next step or meeting.

Find the Place of Comfort

If you are working professionally, with a client, you may have already discussed places of comfort or relaxation with your client during your intake process. This is a wonderful moment to ask your client to bring to mind one of these places (being perfectly aware that her unconscious mind may not bring one of her initial suggestions and may create an alternative location). If you are guiding yourself, simply ask your unconscious mind to bring forth the place of comfort safety and relaxation.

Orient to the Location

Orienting to the location is a key point in this process. Here you ask the client or yourself to step into the situation as fully and completely as possible, using enhanced sensory experience and association. You want your client to feel as though he is truly in the place of comfort, experiencing it as fully as possible in this moment, and highlighting his sensory experience is a great tool for doing this. Using present tense language is the fastest and most effective manner to associate someone into an experience. Asking present tense questions about the client's sensory experience will help to fill out the landscape for the client. For example: You can begin to ask questions such as, "Where *are* you?" and "What are you *seeing* on your left? Turn to your right and notice what you are *hearing*."

If working with a client, it is important to allow her to have her own personal experience at this point. Be aware of making suggestions that may lead her or that could alter her internal landscape. For example: We would not ask or suggest something like, "Feel the warm breeze." We do not know if the client is experiencing a warm breeze, and if we suggest it, the unconscious mind may well bring it forth. A better question would be, "What is the temperature like?" Or, "How is the weather?" By using open-ended questions, we allow the unconscious mind to experience whatever it is experiencing. Ask your client to look in different directions and to become aware of what she can see, what she can hear, and maybe what she can feel in a tactile sense. By orienting her fully to this experience, you are essentially asking the unconscious mind to "come out and play."

It is also important to compound the experience by repeating it back to her. The unconscious mind works very fast and can move from one experience to another in an instant. Repeating your client's phrases helps to stabilize the experience and make it as real as possible.

Here is an example of working with a client to orient to the location.

> Coach: I'd like you to bring to mind a place that is deeply comfortable to you. Maybe it's a place that you are very familiar with or a place you have always wanted to visit. Perhaps it is somewhere that you've seen in a movie, a book, or a magazine. Or maybe you are simply finding yourself in a comfortable place that is new to you. Where are you now?
>
> Client: I'm in a garden.
>
> Coach: You're in a garden. And from where you are in this garden, what can you see in front of you?
>
> Client: I can see a weeping willow tree.
>
> Coach: You can see a weeping willow tree. And is the weeping willow tree moving or still?
>
> Client: The branches are gently moving back and forth.
>
> Coach: So you are in a garden with a weeping willow tree, its branches gently moving. What are you hearing?
>
> Client: I can hear a bird singing somewhere.
>
> Coach: You can hear a bird singing somewhere,

how lovely! And as you turn to your left, what are you aware of now?

Client: I can see roses, a bed of red roses.

Coach: Go over to the red roses. Do they have scent?

Client: Yes, they smell delicious.

Coach: They do smell delicious, don't they! As you turn to look behind you, what's in that direction?

Client: I can see a pond with a fountain in the middle of it. I'd like to go there.

Coach: OK. Go over to the pond with a fountain in it. What's happening now?

Client: I'm holding my hand out and feeling the spray from the fountain.

Coach: So you are in this garden, the weeping willow tree branches waving in the breeze, smelling the delicious scent of the red roses, and feeling the spray from the fountain.

Client: Yes. It's lovely.

Coach: And how are you feeling in your body?

Client: I'm feeling comfortable, warm inside, and deeply relaxed.

Find a Building, a Structure, or a Functional Space

Once your client has fully oriented to this place of relaxation and comfort, it is time to ask the unconscious mind to find a building or structure where the meetings will take place. This is one of the few leading questions that you will pose during this trance. Be aware that a structure may come very quickly to mind, or it may take some time, and more exploration may be required. This building or structure could be absolutely anything: a cottage, tree house, stately home, tent, grand palace. Ask your client what he is seeing, and suggest that this building is a wonderful place, a place of relaxation and a place that he is eager and excited to explore.

It is rare for the unconscious mind not to provide a structure or building at this moment; however, it can happen. The client's unconscious mind may have a meeting place that is outside, so no structure will be found. If you find that your client cannot find a structure, check if the meeting place is an outside one. If the answer is no, then simply ask the client to explore further to find the meeting room.

Find the Meeting Room or Space

Once your client has found the building or structure, ask her to see the doorway or entrance. This is a wonderful moment, for she is about to explore inside the building and find the meeting room. You can frame this moment by saying something like, "And as you enter, you know that your purpose is to find the room where your council will meet. Take a few moments and look around inside. Let me know when you have found a comfortable place for you and your council members to come together."

In the following example we continue with our coach and client working together to find the meeting place.

Coach: So you are in this garden, the weeping willow tree branches waving in the breeze, smelling the delicious scent of the red roses, and feeling the spray from the fountain.

Client: Yes. It's lovely.

Coach: And how are you feeling in your body?

Client: I'm feeling comfortable, warm inside, and deeply relaxed.

Coach: And now I want you to notice there's a building, some kind of structure in the garden. Do you see it?

Client: Yes. There is a small cottage near the weeping willow tree.

Coach: Yes, that's right. There is a small cottage by the weeping willow tree. Go towards this cottage and tell me what you see?

Client: It has roses around the door and is made of stone.

Coach: How lovely! Roses around the door. Now, when you are ready, I want you to enter the cottage knowing that you are going somewhere wonderful, a sanctuary of sorts, the place where you will find the meeting space for you and your council to meet. What's happening now?

Client: I'm inside and it is very modern. Sleek furniture and lots of glass everywhere.

Coach: Fantastic! Now, take a look around, explore for a while, and allow your unconscious mind to lead you to the absolute right place for you to meet your own Council of Inner Advisers. Let me know when you have found it.

Client: Yes, I have it.

Coach: What is it like?

Client: It's a conservatory at the back of the cottage. It has windows all around that look out to the garden. And I can see the willow tree.

Coach: Ahh, a conservatory at the back of the cottage. What else are you seeing?

Client: There are comfortable armchairs, very modern looking with big red cushions around a table.

Coach: And this is the place for you to meet with your council? How do you know?

Client: It just feels right!

Of course, you may find that when working with a client, the client is deeply in trance and finds it more challenging to speak. If this is the case, you will need to ask your client to nod or shake his head to answer your questions, or set up ideomotor signals. You will not be able to echo his responses, but you will have an idea of when he has found a place of comfort and can lead him to explore it in a sensory manner, and you will know when he has found the building and the meeting room.

For example, you could say something like, "When you have found your meeting space, just let me know by nodding your head."

If you are using self-hypnosis, set the intention before going into trance to make this experience as sensory rich as possible, and simply allow your unconscious mind to explore the location until you find your meeting place.

Your meeting space is a place that you will visit and revisit numerous times as you gather your council to meet over the next few days, weeks, months, or even years. During that time, it's normal for the meeting space to morph, change, and evolve. Not only will your council members continue to make added suggestions for changes, but your unconscious mind will make alterations as you go through this process.

In the above coach/client transcript, the client was somewhat surprised when he entered his cottage to find the interior was very sleek and modern. Maybe he had expected a cozy, warm, "grandmotherly" style of interior deign filled with floral wallpaper and chintz-covered sofas. That would certainly have fitted with the stereotypical cottage in a garden with roses round the door image. However, his unconscious mind had something else planned. The client, although somewhat surprised, trusted his unconscious mind enough to go with the flow.

Chapter 7: Introducing Council Members to the Chamber

Now that you have selected your council members and created your meeting space, it is time to introduce each adviser to the place where you will meet together.

When you first invite the council members to the meeting space, some interesting things may happen. I usually ask my members to join me one by one so I can introduce them to the space and show them around. This is also another opportunity to thank them for agreeing to join me on this journey.

During this initial introduction to the space, I ask if this meeting space is good for them. It is at this moment that your advisers may suggest additions, alterations, and changes to make the space more workable for them. As this entire process is intended to be about sharing, it is a good idea to come to a consensus about the meeting space. Be open to any and all suggestions that your councilors may give. I also ask during this initial introduction if this group meeting space is also a good space for the individual council member and me to meet on a one-to-one basis. It is more unusual, in my experience, that the council member wants to meet individually in this space. I have found that the council member usually wishes to meet in a space of her choosing, on her own turf, in a place that is more familiar to her. Once again, trust that your unconscious mind is creating just the right space in which the two of you can have private meetings.

When your adviser invites you to this space, take some time to notice everything about the space. What type of room is it? Is it upstairs or downstairs? What is the lighting like inside? Are there any other objects or items that you unconscious mind seems to focus in on? Remember, this is her space that she has created for the two of you to meet. You may have a sense that it is linked physically to the initial meeting space, almost like an annex or additional room within the house. Alternatively, you may have a sense that it is not physically connected in any way to the council room or initial building. Allow yourself to go with the flow; whatever your unconscious mind brings is right for you. In my experience, meeting in the room of your council members' choosing can bring some wonderful insights into their character, a deeper understanding of who they are as people. It may also offer some hidden gems about their personalities.

I have also found some very interesting things can happen in these moments.

For example: In my personal CIA for writing this book, I met with Stephen King in my own meeting place. He was happy with this place as a general meeting space. However, as soon as I asked if this was also a great place for us to meet privately, we were transported to a room that appeared to be in the office in a house somewhere in the countryside. I had a sense that it was upstairs and that this was the place where Stephen did much of his writing. There was a typewriter on the desk and to its side, a cup of tea.
When my trance finished, I was very curious. I didn't know anything about the author Stephen King; I have never read any of his works. However, the room I had just visited in my mind seemed so real that I decided to Google "Where does Stephen King write?" I checked a number of images, and quite a few of them had strong similarities to the images I had just seen in my trance.

This type of experience is not altogether uncommon. There are two possible explanations for this phenomenon. (I'm sure there are many more that I haven't considered or figured out.)

1. I believe that as human beings, we are all interconnected on some level. By using trance, the unconscious mind, and the CIA process, we are able to tap into this connection, which then provides details about our council members that we could not have known consciously.

2. Our unconscious mind remembers vast amounts of information that we are unaware we have. I'm sure that over the years, I have probably seen clips, articles, and interviews of Stephen King. Not having a particular interest in his genre of writing, I probably paid little or no conscious attention. However, my unconscious mind has taken in enough of these details for them to be accessed through trance.

So is it some kind of telecommunication, mental transportation, psychic insight, or unique ability of the unconscious mind to store and recall hitherto unknown facts? I don't know. All I do know is that this happens more frequently than I can begin to explain. So be ready for the unexpected, and be comfortable in the knowledge that the unconscious mind is a powerful ally.

Visualizing Your Council of Advisers

Go into a trance and take yourself to your meeting place. Invite the members of the council into the space one by one. Greet each council member, show him or her around the space, and ask if this is the right place to meet. The advisers may make requests in regard to the space.

For example: One may ask for chalkboards or flip charts to be available. Another may ask for an outdoor space. A third may ask for a table. A fourth may wish to add a kitchen for refreshments and more casual encounters. A fifth may add a space to move around and physically enact the ideas being discussed. A sixth may add a tower to get a different perspective. And so on. Allow the space to flexibly change.

The Council of Advisers will now meet for its first meeting. Notice how each of the advisers looks as he walks into the space, and how they all gather at the place where the meeting is to take place. Again, if you are working with a client, ask her to describe in detail. Continue to note (or describe) how each of council member is dressed and how he walks, talks, and interacts.

Thank each of the advisers for coming; explain to each member why she is here; and ask each of the advisers to impart her particular wisdom.

The following is from my personal experience of my CIA for writing this book. In this example, I introduce Eleanor Roosevelt to the meeting space.

> I invited Eleanor Roosevelt to the white pavilion, and I noticed as she climbed the steps that the figure I was looking at was black and white. It struck me as slightly unusual although understandable. Every image or picture I recall seeing of Mrs. Roosevelt has been in black and white. I asked if she could change the color, and magically she transformed before my eyes into color. She was wearing a navy blue coat, navy blue hat with pink flowers on it, and pale blue gloves. On the crook of her arm, she carried a black handbag similar to the style my grandmother had, with a clasp on the top, wore sensible shoes, and smelled like lily-of-the-valley perfume. Mrs. Roosevelt removed her coat and

gloves and was wearing a blue and pink floral day dress.

She immediately asked, "Is this where you write? Because this is not the right place for you to be writing anything. It's too relaxed."

I was a little startled and smiled and said, "No, I don't write here. This is where we get together as the council, a comfortable place where we can relax, where everyone is equal and we can share ideas and suggestions."

"That's perfect" Eleanor said. "So where do you write?" she asked.

"Well I write anywhere I want," I said.

"You don't have an office with a typewriter?" she asked.

"No" I replied, "I have my laptop computer, and I also use Dragon Dictate on my iPhone."
Eleanor Roosevelt looked at me blankly. She had no idea to what I was referring. I pulled my iPhone out of my pocket, tapped the app for dictation, and showed her how by simply speaking into my phone this particular app will translate my spoken word into written text.

"Well, that is truly amazing," said Eleanor Roosevelt.

"You really can write anywhere and whenever inspiration strikes. However, you still need to have a special place in order to write."

I wasn't quite sure what she meant. I assumed she meant a particular room, maybe a personal desk, my own sacred space for writing, or something else.

Mrs. Roosevelt must've read my mind because she immediately said, "It doesn't have to be a physical space. You need the right space in your mind to write. Once you have that, then everything will be easy."

I understood exactly what she meant, although consciously I'm not aware of exactly where that space is.

"Oh, we are going to get this book written so easily, Sarah," said Mrs. Roosevelt.

I smiled and said, "Well, that's the reason I asked you here, to give me the push that I need, the encouragement, the 'just-do-it-ness' to get this book written."

"Then that's what we'll do," replied Eleanor Roosevelt.

I then asked Eleanor if the white pavilion was the best place for us to meet. She smiled and said she liked it fine; however, she preferred the drawing room for our private meetings. As soon as she said this, we were transported to the elegant drawing room where we had taken tea together. This time there were two comfortable sofas and a low table set with tea. Once again, Mrs. Roosevelt was pouring tea from a fine bone china teapot.

"Oh, I do love this time of day when I can simply relax, but I always keep it to a strict 15 minutes. Keeping a tight schedule is vitally important," she said to me with a knowing smile.

Chapter 8: The First Council Meeting

By now, you or your client will have chosen the council members either consciously or unconsciously, conducted interviews, and may have spent some time meeting with them individually on a one-on-one basis to ensure you have made the right selection. The meeting space will have been established both where you will meet as a group, as well as any additions or private meeting spaces. This process may have already taken a number of days or weeks. It may have been a series of trances or possibly has been established in just one session.

It is now time to hold your first meeting as a CIA. This meeting is an opportunity for council members to get to know one another, to establish their specific role and purpose on the committee, and to begin to work cohesively as a group.

This step is a relatively easy one, one that is often fun and exciting. The first meeting usually feels as though the entire process is really beginning to come together, and it often feels like the real work can begin.

You can simply take yourself into trance. (If you are working with a client, lead the client into a light trance.) Suggest that you want to be in your meeting space. Once you are associated into being in your meeting space, you can bring to mind your council.

Watch as the members of your council arrive in the council chamber. How do they walk in? Notice their posture, breathing, facial expressions, and gestures. Notice how they walk. Are they walking in alone or with other members of the council? Do they speak as they walk in? Where do they choose to sit? Take some time to fully observe, and when ready, call the meeting to order.

It is usual at the first meeting to ask each individual council member to take a few moments to introduce himself and to share the reason he has been selected to be a member of the council. You (or your client) are the leader of this meeting, the chairman of the board, and you decide whose turn it is to speak, how long each member may have to speak, and exactly how this initial meeting will be run.

You may wish to give each council member a set time to introduce herself. You may wish your council members to mingle first before settling down. Perhaps you will have snacks and light refreshments available so that your council members meet in a more casual setting first before calling the meeting to order.

There are many options for you at this moment; however, it is common to simply ask each member to introduce himself and the role he will be playing. At some point—either before you ask the members to introduce themselves or after they have done so—it is important for you (or the client) to take a moment to thank the council members for agreeing to be part of this council to help to guide you towards your specific goal. Depending on the time available, you may wish to pose an initial question to your council to open up a discussion. There are numerous ways in which you can ask for guidance from your CIA. (We discuss these further in a later chapter.)

Here is an example of the first meeting of my CIA for writing this book.

As I opened my mind to setting up the first meeting, I entered my white pavilion and noticed that to my left were four white two-seater sofas arranged in a rectangle around a low white wooden coffee table. I sat on one sofa with the entrance steps to the pavilion on my right, and I asked the members of my inner council to enter the pavilion and to take a seat. I didn't place them in any particular area or arrange the seating in any way. I simply allowed the members of my council to choose their own seats.

Einstein and Steve Jobs took the sofa to my immediate right, Einstein closest to me. Opposite me at the far end of the coffee table sat Shawn and Stephen King. The two ladies took the sofa on my left, with Eleanor Roosevelt closest to me and Victoria Wood on her left. Interestingly, for many of our subsequent meetings, everybody took the same seats.

I welcomed everyone and thanked them all once again for agreeing to be members of my Council of Inner Advisers and for their guidance and support for me in the process of writing this book. I then asked everyone to introduce himself or herself starting with Einstein.

Einstein simply smiled at everyone and said, "Hello, I'm Albert Einstein, and I'm here to help Sarah in any way I can. She has asked me specifically to focus on creativity, thinking outside the box, and in generating new and different ideas."

Everyone smiled and nodded.

Steve Jobs then said, "Hi, I'm Steve. Sarah has asked me to be here to help her with focus, although I think I can bring a great deal more to this process than simply that."

I smiled at Shawn next, and he said, "I'm here to help Sarah just get this book done" I smiled recognizing Shawn's "straight to the pointedness."

Stephen King was next, and he said, "Thank you, Sarah, for inviting me to this council. I can bring a wealth of experience, as I have spent my entire life writing, even before I knew I was a writer."

I smiled and thanked him.

Victoria Wood then took the floor and said, "Hullo," in a strong British Northern accent. "I'm here to have fun, to help Sarah to have fun, and we can all have fun in this process, can't we?"
I smiled and nodded and noticed that everyone else was smiling and agreeing.

Just as Eleanor Roosevelt was about to speak, Einstein interjected and said, "Oh, here comes bossy boots."

To which Eleanor replied, "No, not to you, Mr. Einstein, only to Sarah. She is the one we are all here for after all. It is my role to motivate her and to ensure that she has the correct incentive to get this book written."

Mr. Einstein smiled and nodded and said, "Yes, that's what we're here for. I was just having a bit of fun!"

I then thanked everyone for introducing themselves and said that we would undoubtedly enjoy working together as a team. I explained again that we would meet sometimes as an entire group, possibly in small groups, or even individually, and that at this point, I was uncertain as to exactly how we would meet. I asked if everyone was comfortable with having a very flexible schedule, and everyone agreed. I then asked everyone to give me one piece of advice, one tidbit, one takeaway for me as I was starting out in this writing process. We went around the group in the same order starting with Einstein.

Instantly, we were all in an old, beautiful, high-ceiling library. The kind of library you may see in a stately home, with shelves of books reaching from floor to ceiling, comfortable chairs arranged around the room, and ladders attached to the walls to slide easily from one shelf to another.

"I have brought you here for a reason," said Einstein.

"Each and every one of these books was written by someone. These books are filled with someone's ideas, thoughts, stories, theories, so precious to them they wanted to share them with the world. Each and every one of these writers had their own method of writing, their own process, went through their own struggles. Some of these books were written very easily, the words flowing from mind to page. Some authors probably struggled to get the words down, and their books may have taken years to write. Each author went through a period of transformation; each one broke their own rules. So I say to you, Sarah, as my piece of advice: break your own rules."

I wasn't certain exactly what Einstein meant by this, but I trusted that my unconscious mind would make sense of it.

Suddenly, we were back in the white pavilion sitting around the coffee table.

Steve Jobs pulled out an iPhone, held it up, and said to everyone, "This is my library. Remember that the readers of today and tomorrow will access books in ways we haven't even begun to think about yet. My advice to you is to keep your eye on the prize and set yourself targets that you can easily reach. Oh, and one more thing: each day set yourself a target that you can't reach."

I thanked Steve and asked Shawn for his advice, and in typical Shawn fashion he simply said, "Just write, just write something, just start and the rest will flow easily."

I smiled having heard this advice from Shawn before I knew he was absolutely right. I turned to Stephen King, and I asked him for his nugget of advice.

He smiled and said, "Keep your reader in mind." Short and simple and absolutely true.

I then asked Victoria Wood for her advice as I started out on this new project. She smiled and said, "Smile often when you're writing."

This seems to make perfect sense to me because I know that when we smile our brain releases dopamine. This is a feel-good neurotransmitter, and feeling good while writing is a wonderful thing.

Finally I asked Eleanor Roosevelt for her piece of wisdom. She said, "A little every day." Short and sweet.

I thanked everyone for their advice, knowing that I would take this forward as I began the process of writing.

Chapter 9:
Interacting with Your Council

Now that your Council of Inner Advisers has been established and has met for the first time, you have a wide variety of options available to you as to how you interact and use your council.

Basic Method

The basic message is to simply interact with your council just as a regular "real-life" council or board would interact. You act as chairperson, posing the questions and directing how they may answer. Perhaps you will select an individual and ask her for an opinion. At other times, you may open the question to the entire floor. The basic method is simple and is usually one that most people are familiar with. Of course, you are also able to set up individual meetings, subcommittees, and working groups and interact with them in this manner. You may also wish to change your meeting location or add addition rooms or space.

One-Word Message

A simple and powerful way to use your council is the one-word message. Pose a question or topic to your council, and ask your council members for one word that encapsulates his or her opinion. This is often useful after a period of deep discussion as a final-word exercise. These words then form the basis of your guidance. This is a very useful message to use just before going to sleep. You can ask your unconscious mind to make any decisions and to give further guidance whilst dreaming.

Here is an example of using the one-word message technique with my CIA for Writing.

> I went into trance just before falling asleep and called a brief meeting of the council. I explained that I was doing well with writing the book and simply wanted a word of encouragement from each of them.
>
> Eleanor Roosevelt went first and said, "fortitude".
>
> Victoria Wood smiled and said, "Mr. Rotivator." (There was a comedy sketch years ago in the UK where two older ladies talk about a TV fitness instructor nicknamed Mr. Motivator. In the sketch the two ladies call him Mr. Rotivator. This sketch always made me giggle.)
>
> Stephen King simply said, " Strength."
> And Shawn said, "Moving."
>
> Steve Jobs made a "whooosh" sound and moved his hand in a forward motion.
>
> Einstein nodded and said, "Understanding."
>
> I thanked everyone, took a moment to write these words down, and drifted off to sleep.

Giving Symbols

This process is similar to the one-word message technique. Instead of asking each council member to provide a word, you ask the council members to give a symbolic item. We know the unconscious mind communicates with images, pictures, and symbols, and this can be a deeply profound and hypnotic interaction.

The following is an example from my CIA.

> I took myself into trance and then to my white pavilion. The council members were already seated in the usual seats. I thanked them for their help thus far in writing this book, and explained that I felt I was at a crucial point in my writing. I had written over 20,000 words and hoped I was about halfway through. I wanted to maintain the motivation, direction, and focus necessary to complete the book in a timely manner. I explained that I would ask each member to provide me with a symbol or an object to help motivate me, sharpen my focus, and keep me on track.
>
> I asked Stephen King first, and he immediately gave me a small golden anchor. It looked like a charm for a bracelet or possibly a pendant from a necklace. I thanked him and placed it on the table before me.
>
> Shawn then gave me a muffin in a colorful purple wrapper. It looked a dark color, possibly a whole wheat or chocolate muffin. Once again, I thanked him and then turned to Steve Jobs.

He gave me the blade of grass that he had been playing with when we first met in the meadow outside the white pavilion.

Einstein then gave me a ball of energy. It appeared almost as a hologram of white and yellow light between his hands.

Eleanor Roosevelt then turned and gave me a small glass thimble, and Victoria Wood gave a black beret.

I took some time to look at the six items on the table in front of me. I then took each object one by one asking my unconscious mind to provide me with some deeper understanding as to the meaning of the symbol. I was well aware that the unconscious mind may or may not provide me with a word to explain the symbol, but I was comfortable with that.

I took the golden anchor in my hand and instantly had an understanding of anchoring myself to the outcome. I took the muffin into myself symbolically. It felt comfortable; however, I had no further meaning. I held the blade of grass in my hand and allowed that to give me its meaning.

Instantly I could hear Steve Jobs saying, "Every tiny thing is important. Every blade of grass has its worth."

I placed my hands around the ball of energy and instantly felt its meaning. It was the sense of pure potentiality. I held the small glass thimble in my hand and was somewhat curious as to what the meaning may be. A thimble seems a very old-fashioned tool, and I don't think I've ever seen a glass thimble in the real world. However, as soon as I picked it up, I could hear Eleanor Roosevelt saying something about it being a sign of a woman working hard, and the fact that it was glass represented beauty. As I looked at the black beret that Victoria Wood gave me, it immediately brought a smile to my face.

"That's what it's for," quipped Victoria instantly, "to make you smile." One of her most famous comedy characters would often wear a beret, and this represented continuing to have fun and smile through the process.

I then took all the objects into myself, into my heart, my soul, and my being knowing that my unconscious mind would make even more meaning from these items as I moved forward with the writing of this book.

Hot-Seating

When using this method, select one member of your council to take the "hot seat." You may wish to alter the seating arrangements for this so that the adviser selected to sit on the hot seat is on one side of the table or space with the other council members on the opposite side. This is an opportunity for everyone on the council to ask questions specifically aimed at this one adviser. This method can be used to further develop a plan, gain more background information about a member, or study one person's behavior or motivations. This method can offer a deeper level of connection with and understanding of a council member.

Decision Ally

The decision ally is an interesting method for helping you to come to a conclusion or make a decision. Occasionally, you may find that despite good discussions, you are still unable to reach a decision and that you are being given conflicting advice from different council members. This particular method works very well if there are an equal number of members on either side of an argument.

Ask the members to stand in two rows, organizing themselves so that those council member on one side of the argument stand in one row and the others stand in the opposite row. Ask the two rows to face each other. This will make the "tunnel" down which you will walk. Take a step down the center of the tunnel, and stop alongside each pair. Each time you stop, the person on your right will give a sentence to support his view and the person to your left will give his point of view. Once you have heard the position from either side, move to the space between the second pair and hear both sides of the argument from these two. Continue until you have reached the end of your tunnel. Traditionally, at the end of the tunnel, it is time for you to make a decision. This can be a useful moment to use just before going to sleep and asking the unconscious mind to make the decision during sleep incubation.

Sit in My Chair

This is a great way to interact with your council members and begin to see things from a different perspective. At any time— after a discussion, midconversation, or simply as an exercise in and of itself—you can ask the members to vacate the room and then sit in the chair or space that your adviser sits or stands in. You may find that your council members take the same positions at each meeting and, therefore, their personalities and characteristics have become synonymous with that position. By "sitting in my chair" you will begin to get a sense of seeing things through your advisers' eyes.

Here is an extract from my CIA of the sit-in-my-chair method. Up to this point, we had discussed possible color options for the front cover, and I had asked all the members to leave a copy of the book and cover idea on their chair before they left room.

> I wanted to do the "to-sit-in-my-chair" exercise. In this exercise, I would sit in each person's chair and take on his or her perspective and point of view and look at the book cover they had suggested.

> I moved to Eleanor Roosevelt's chair and picked up the copy of the book to look at. It had a navy blue front cover that looked rather mundane and dull. I put the book down and moved to Victoria Wood's chair. I picked up the yellow book and interestingly enough the title kept changing to a book I hope to write in the future! From here, I moved to Stephen King's seat and held the blood red book. I liked the dynamic impact of this book. I moved to Shawn's seat, and here the book I picked up changed into a wide variety of different colors and did not settle on one in particular. As soon as I sat in Steve Jobs's seat and picked up the black and gray book, I knew instantly that it didn't work for me. The last seat was Albert Einstein's, and I saw the royal blue cover of the book and liked it instantly.

> I decided to allow my unconscious mind, through sleep incubation, to process the discussion and decide which color the book would be.

Keeping Records

Keeping letters or diaries is something that our ancestors have done for thousands of years. Famous people, presidents, and people of note have been known to keep journals that later inform our understanding of them, of the culture, and of society at their time. Oscar Wilde, the famous playwright, is purported to have said, "I never travel without my diary. One should always have something sensational to read on the train."

More recently there has been increasing evidence to support the idea that journaling has a positive impact on us and on our well-being. I have found it not only useful but also insightful to journal my experiences when using the CIA.

The CIA process is a very hypnotic one. Just as dreams that seem vivid in the moment of dreaming quickly become simply fragments of an idea before we have even got out of bed, the hypnotic experience can also fade quickly. As hypnosis is an unconscious process, we are often unaware of every aspect of our trance experience. It can be useful with the CIA Pattern to write down what we recall. This provides us with further opportunities to revisit certain aspects, to formulate further questions, and to consolidate our learnings.

Record keeping can be done in a number of ways. You can use a traditional journaling method of having a particular journal and immediately after meeting with your council writing down your experience. Another method that I have found very useful is to use a voice dictate app. These are readily available and can be downloaded onto your smartphone. The beauty of this sort of technology is in its simplicity. As you are coming out of trance, it is easy to record your experience by simply speaking into the phone. Your words are translated into text that you can then email to yourself. I know that I can speak faster than I can write in longhand and faster than I type on my computer, so the voice dictation app can capture my thoughts and record my experience before the details fade away.

Automatic Writing

Another method of recording your experience is to use automatic writing. This experience is not simply recalling your trance experience but is used while in the trance experience to record the discussions and to take notes. However, it requires a little more setup and preparation than remembering to voice dictate or write in a journal.

Before you settle down into a trance, make sure you have a pen and a pad of paper nearby. Hold the pen in your hand with the tip resting on the paper. Whilst meeting with your council members, you may take on the role of secretary as well as facilitator. Instruct your unconscious mind to keep records of what is being said, just as a secretary would take the minutes of the meeting.

Another method is to do something similar from the point of view of one of your council members. Let's say you have the actor Tom Hanks on your council and you wish to experience the discussion or conversation from his perspective.

- Before you go into trance, make sure you have a notepad and pen in hand ready to do your automatic writing.
- In trance, go to your meeting space and meet your council. Ask Tom Hanks if he is willing for you to do this process.
- If he is, then thank him and ask him to merge with you. This will be as though Tom Hanks were stepping into you.
- As the meeting begins, instruct your unconscious mind and your hand to write thoughts and experiences from Tom Hanks's point of view.

- At the end of the meeting—and this is vitally important—ask Tom Hanks to take every part of him that is "him."
- Ensure that you are fully and completely yourself before emerging from trance. [2]

---

[2] This is effectively a Reverse Deep Trance Identification. We will discuss this process further in our book *Deep Trance Identification* by Shawn Carson, Jess Marion, with John Overdurf.

Chapter 10: Dream Incubation

Humanity has been fascinated by dreams since the beginning of time. There is evidence from the Babylonians, the Greeks, and the Egyptians that dreams were interpreted and thought to be divine interventions or even supernatural communications. Dreams have long been interpreted, analyzed, and read by those with unique and special abilities. In the 20th century, dreams moved into the arena of psychoanalysis. Sigmund Freud and Carl Jung used dreams extensively to understand their patients. Freud believed dreams represented unfulfilled wishes and latent desires. Jung believed dreams to be archetypal symbols and thought that dreams were a way to access the collective conscious.

More recently neuroscience has indicated that dreams play an important part in practicing skills, learning, problem solving, memory construction, and consolidation.

Undoubtedly, there is much more to be learned about how we dream, why we dream, the function of dreams, and what purpose they serve. But this much we know: we all dream. Every night. Some people are able to recollect their dreams in vivid detail. Some believe they never dream. Others can recall only fragments of dreams only for those fragments to disappear within moments.

Most people will tell of dreams that include references to events, objects, happenings that have been in their real-life experience. Often these normal, everyday experiences are coupled with surreal, obscure, or unusual events, making dreams an art form unlike any other. People often dream fantastical, random story lines that seem to bring together polar opposite themes and do not follow a regular story structure or plot line. Other people recall dreams that are more mundane and seem to have some sense of purpose.

What we do know is that we dream for around two hours each night. These two hours are spread over a number of sleep cycles, each cycle lasting around 90 minutes. Within each sleep cycle are four stages plus rapid eye movement (REM) sleep. We dream most frequently during REM sleep.

We experience two types of dreams during the cycles: dreams for our emotional well-being and dreams for integrating learning. Dreams associated with our emotional well-being are a wonderful opportunity for us to reset, to work through emotional issues, and to let go of any negative emotions that do not serve us.

Maybe you have had the experience of having had a bad day and going to bed feeling out of sorts or emotionally drained, but on waking the next day you feel reenergized, revitalized, and refreshed having let go of whatever was bothering you. This is because while you were dreaming, your unconscious mind was able to work through the issues, emotions, and states using the modality of dreams.

When we are sleeping, we also rewire the brain. New information is being linked to existing neural networks, thereby creating new neural pathways of learning, consolidation, and integration of new skills. It is no coincidence that babies sleep for an inordinate amount of time. This is the period of the most rapid brain growth, and it is said that we as humans learn more in the first year of life than at any other stage. So while your baby is sleeping, she is learning and growing. And we continue to do this throughout our life.

Maybe you can recall a time when you were planning something new and your dreams were filled with practicing this new skill, reliving your experiences, and trying out new ways of using your skill. One of my hobbies is singing. I know that whenever I am learning a new piece of music, invariably I wake with specific fragments of the new song playing in my head. I know that I had been singing in my sleep, practicing the new skill, and consolidating my knowledge. Of course, we are talking about dreams, so inevitably some fantastical, weird, unusual aspects show up in my dreams too. In fact, I recall having a singing dream and somehow my cat was singing my new aria with me!

When using dream incubation with your CIA, you are using the natural ability of the brain to integrate information, skills, guidance, knowledge, and new learnings you acquire through interacting with your council. You will also be allowing your unconscious mind to make decisions, play with options, and come to agreement about issues you have brought to your council.

Dreams also have a therapeutic effect allowing you to deal with any emotions that surround the issues you are discussing with your council. So whether you are using your council to guide you through a specific issue or to give direction in a more general manner, you will undoubtedly experience profound emotional change through this practice.

Your council members are fully rounded human beings, and even though you are bringing them to mind through a hypnotic process, and have probably selected them to be on your council because of one specific trait or characteristic, it is impossible for you not to see other sides of their character and personality. You may find that you are also influenced by these other positive characteristics.

For example: You may have selected Pablo Picasso to assist you with creativity on your council. You may find not only that your creative ability has increased but also that you have taken on the focus, dedication, and diligence that Picasso imparted. You may also find that your unconscious mind may have taken on the creative abilities of others who have not been selected for your council but have demonstrated a great creativity in their lives. So you may find that you have been dreaming about Michelangelo, Coco Chanel, or Walt Disney to aid in your development of your own personal creativity.

With dream incubation, you directionalize your dreams (or those of your clients) so that you can embody the skills, knowledge, and understanding of your CIA members as well as allowing your unconscious mind to make decisions based on the advice and guidance evoked through your council meetings.

Please be aware that we are not instructing ourselves (or our clients) as to the specifics of what to dream about. We are only informing the unconscious mind that we wish to explore further these areas or questions to which we would like answers or decisions that may require a solution. We are asking the unconscious mind to explore and play with these aspects while we sleep. We are simply sowing the seeds and allowing the unconscious mind to help grow the solutions, answers, and ideas.

Dream incubation is a relatively simple process, yet it requires some setup. Following we explain how to utilize a dream incubation both for a client and when using self-hypnosis.

Using Dream Incubation with a Client

Using dream incubation with a client is relatively simple, as the client is likely to be already in trance or at least very "trancy." This means you simply give posthypnotic suggestions to your client. You are likely to do this towards the end of a session, and it can be used for any aspect of setting up the CIA or working with your client's council. You can use dream incubation to help your client to select council members, select a meeting place, or have meetings or discussions with council and to make conclusions and find answers. This process will also help the client's unconscious mind to remember to take any learnings from the experience and integrate them on a deeper level through dreams.

We keep these posthypnotic suggestions extremely open. There are a few reasons for this. The first is that your client's unconscious mind already knows how to dream in a way that is ecological for your client. We do not wish to alter this in any way other than to suggest or directionalize the mind as to what to dream about. The client's unconscious mind knows far more about your client than you, as a coach, will ever know. We have to trust that the unconscious mind will provide the client whatever is needed during her dream experience.

The second reason for keeping suggestions open and indirect is because of the individual way that your client experiences dreams. Some people dream very elaborate and surreal dreams. Some people may have only fragments of dreams. Others forget their dreams and think they have had no dreams at all. If you, as coach or hypnotist, give very specific suggestions about a dream, and your client does not experience this specific style of dream or outcome, the client may believe that this process does not work. We want to give our clients every opportunity to succeed, and keeping these posthypnotic suggestions generally means that whatever your client experiences is absolutely right for her.

Giving posthypnotic suggestions can be short and simple, for example:

> "And when you go home tonight, you will sleep,
> and when you sleep you will dream. And in that

dream your unconscious mind can continue the conversations you have had here today, offering additional insight, and integrate all of the learnings you have made. Now, you may be aware of the dreams or maybe the unconscious mind will choose to forget. Whichever way is absolutely right for you, and you will know that your unconscious mind is making deep and profound change as you sleep and dream."

In this example, notice that the suggestions are very open even to the extent that the client may or may not remember the dream. You are leaving this open for your client's unconscious mind to make whatever meaning out of it that is right for him. Of course, you can become more elaborate with your wording using such tools as double blinds and universal quantifiers so that whatever your client experiences during the night—whether he remembers the dream or not—upon awakening the next day he will have an understanding that the unconscious mind has made a change and has gone through a process that is beneficial for him.

Here is a suggestion developed by John Overdurf that we have used frequently with students and clients.

"You have had many experiences today, you have learned new things, and your mind is opening to new experiences. Eventually tonight, when you go home, you will go to bed ... and when you go to bed, you will sleep, and when you sleep, you will dream. Now, I don't know what kind of dream you will have. Some people have exciting dreams, some people have boring and mundane dreams, some people have Technicolor dreams, and others black-and-white dreams. Some people dream with a cast of thousands, or just a few, or you may think that you have no dreams at all and let that want to be a sign of the changes taking place on the deepest unconscious level."

Self-Hypnosis and Dream Incubation

We can break this process down into three easy steps. The first step is to ensure that the unconscious mind is ready for dreaming. The second step comes at the moment you are falling asleep at night and wish to directionalize and initiate the dream. The third step comes in the morning as you awaken and record the dream in a dream journal.

Step 1: Preparing for the Dream

In preparation for your dream, you will need to both set your intention and prepare your body and mind for your dream experience.

Setting your intention is easy. Take a moment to consider a recent experience with your CIA, a discussion, a question, maybe a symbol that appeared that you would like to explore more. Maybe your intention is concerned with finding the correct meeting space or having an internal meeting with one of your advisers. You may have had a recent council meeting to discuss one specific point and wish to set this is your dream intention. Whatever your intention, we suggest that you write it down in a dream journal. Write it down as a title or a question, keeping it concise and simple.

In preparation for your dream, we suggest that you eat sensibly the evening before the dream. Avoid overeating and eating any food that may be too rich or cause discomfort. Also avoid alcohol. We also suggest you avoid any activities that may overstimulate the unconscious mind for a period before going to bed. These may include surfing the web, playing computer games, or watching movies, television, or news programs.

Instead, we suggest you spend some time relaxing. This can include taking a warm bath or shower or spending some time in meditation or mindful breathing.

Step 2: Falling Asleep

If you have set your intention early in the day, this step is very important. If, however, you are doing your dream intention whilst in bed, you may find that you simply go off to sleep and do not need this step. This protocol is based on Shawn's experience with lucid dreaming and shared dreaming.

Once in bed, allow your vision to expand so that you can see the entire space around you—or would be able to see it if it were not dark. Allow your eyes to close while in this peripheral vision state. The more familiar you become with this state, the more easily you will be able to access it with your eyes closed.

Once again, bring to mind your meeting room. Pay attention to all the details that you see. Are you with your council members or alone? Are you noticing anything new or different? Are you somewhere new? Make this as full a sensory experience as possible. When you are ready, simply ask your question. It is very possible that you will drift off to sleep during this exercise for a moment or two. You may even find that you fall asleep completely. If you do, you can simply repeat this process from beginning, expanding your awareness, including all of your senses, taking yourself to your meeting place, and posing the question.

Set your intention, go into trance, ask your unconscious mind to dream, bring to mind your meeting space, and ask the question. Listen to your council members discuss the question as you drift off to sleep.

As soon as you wake in the morning, and before you get out of bed, recall the dreams you have just experienced. Thank your unconscious mind, and record your dreams in your dream journal. It is a good idea to have your dream journal and a pen close at hand, right at your bedside, so that you can write your dream down immediately. As we know, dreams can fade in an instant, so it is a good idea to have your journal close by.

Dream Analysis

You may find the answer to your question has been clearly addressed, and you may find that you awaken with clarity about a decision. But you may also find that you have had a dream that appears unrelated. Whatever your dream is, write it down so that you can begin to analyze it. If your answer is clear and a decision made, it will take very little analyzing! However, if you seem to have had a normal or surreal dream, this dream may take a little more time to figure out. If you are familiar with doing any internal work, you know that your unconscious mind speaks in symbols and images. Creating a good relationship with your unconscious mind is vital for this kind of work, and you may rest assured that, even if you do not fully understand the symbolism within your dream, your unconscious mind knows exactly what it is for.

There are tens of thousands of dream interpretation and analysis books available, and it is beyond the scope of this book to go into much depth as to what the symbolism within a dream may mean. We do, however, recommend the excellent book *Dreaming Realities* by John Overdurf and Julie Silverthorn.

Dream incubation is a vital part of the CIA process. We encourage you to use it often right from the beginning of the process of selecting your members all the way through to the various meetings you have. As with anything, the more you practice, the easier it becomes.

Chapter 11: NLP, Hypnosis, and the CIA Pattern

You now have your council established and have begun to interact and meet. Hopefully, you are using dream incubation to further consolidate your learnings and are keeping records of your interactions, outcomes, dreams, and moments of insight. In keeping with Napoleon Hill's original idea of creating a council of advisers, using trance and dreams, we have given details as to how to create the council and the meeting space and how to interact with your CIA. Napoleon Hill mentioned very little about how he did this in his book *Think and Grow Rich*, so we have given our own explanations and details for each step of the method.

In the following chapters, we move to a different perspective. Here, for those readers familiar with NLP and hypnosis, we outline a few patterns and demonstrate how to use them in combination with your Council of Inner Advisers. These NLP and hypnosis patterns underlie the CIA Pattern in that they provide us with the opportunity to actively engage with the parts of us represented by our individual council members.

The New Behavior Generator

The New Behavior Generator utilizes a very familiar skill known as *implicit modeling.* Implicit modeling can be thought of as copying. If you have ever watched children play, you may have noticed that they are likely to play at being characters from movies or video games or impersonating the adults around them. Their make-believe games consist of mimicking or copying the behaviors they have seen, including facial expressions, movements, language, words, and phrases. If you are a parent, it is likely that you have seen or heard some of your own body language, behaviors, or phrases come out of the mouths of your children while they are playing!

This is a natural way of learning, and it is hardwired into our brains. Remember, mirror neurons and the concept that when we see an action performed our brain reacts as if we were actually doing the action ourselves. This provides an initial experience of performing the action that the brain uses as a reference or model before actually doing it.

I remember, as a child, I would play at being teacher. I was usually Mrs. Holgarth or Miss Austin or whichever teacher I had that year. I would gather all my dolls and soft toys to be my students and would spend hours in my bedroom (or classroom) teaching them, reprimanding them, taking them on school trips, giving them homework. All of this was based on copying the actions and words of the teachers I had experienced in my own school, on TV, or from films.

Now, you may remember doing something very similar in your childhood and can recall a time when you pretended to be somebody else. Perhaps you had been to see a film and wanted to be the hero or heroine. Maybe it was a football player, an athlete, or some other sports star. Maybe you were a rock star, a film or TV star. Maybe it was a teacher or someone else at school you admired. I don't know, but I do know that we have all had these experiences.

Take a moment now and think of an experience just like that time when you really liked a person and just wanted to be like that person. A time when you pretended to be her, to be someone whom you truly admired, someone who was your hero. Remember what it feels like now as you step back into this experience. Feel what it feels like to have this sense of openness, a child-like openness to becoming another person for a while. Be aware of how it feels to have this child-like curiosity about how things are done, a child-like belief that you can become someone else for a time. Back then it wasn't really necessary to understand; it was more important to just do. As you look at your hero, notice how she is standing, moving, breathing. See her facial expression, and remember what it was like to find yourself becoming this person, stepping into her shoes, seeing out of her eyes, feeling what she is feeling, saying what she is saying, believing that you can do anything that your hero can do.

Implicit modeling relies on the fact that the physiology, facial expression, posture, and other features reflect the underlying state that a person is experiencing. While it is not necessarily true that adopting all of these aspects will replicate that state, there is a link between the two. Research has shown that the mind controls every aspect of our body: our unconscious breathing, our heartbeat, the regeneration of our cells, and every other physical process. *How* we think, and *what* we think, causes our body to respond according to those specific thoughts. In fact, there is an entire area of neuroscience called *embodied cognition* devoted to this idea. Research has discovered that when read an emotionally charged word, we begin to feel or become that emotion. The same is true if we read an action phrase like *I am walking*. The body begins to act as if it were about to walk. When we make images in our mind's eye of us holding our body in a certain position or having a particular facial expression, our body automatically begins to adopt that same physiology or facial expression. This is one reason why putting our awareness and attention on our center of gravity causes our balance to improve. Or thinking about a golden thread attached from the spine up through the crown of the head and upwards to the sky causes the spine to lengthen.

Our body responds to the thoughts we are having. It responds to our self talk, as well as to the images and pictures we create inside the mind. If we tell ourselves that we feel shy, our physiology begins to reflect this. The same is true if we tell ourselves that we feel confident; the body and physiology begin to reflect the confidence.

Now, the interesting thing is that this also works if we imagine another person. We know that seeing someone else move activates the mirror neurons in our brain. So if we see someone walking with confidence, this fires off the mirror neurons and confidence networks within our brain.

The New Behavior Generator is a pattern that utilizes implicit modeling. It can be used powerfully to enhance our understanding and experience of our council members.

The Steps of the New Behavior Generator

1. See your selected council member in front of you. Focus on his or her physiology, particularly posture, gestures, and facial expression.

2. Begin to mimic or copy these movements and facial expressions as closely as possible.

3. Become aware of any specific repeated gestures.

4. When you feel in sync with your council member, float into the image as though you have stepped inside your council member, and experience her from the inside out.

5. Continue to experience the council member, and when you are ready, step out and take a look once again at the image of your council member. Maybe you would like to make this picture brighter or bigger. Make any changes you wish, and when you are ready, step back into your council member and feel how good it feels. When you are ready, step out.

This is the basic New Behavior Generator Pattern. We can extend and enhance this pattern by taking these additional steps.

6. See your council member in front of you, and make the picture big and bright. Step in again and experience him from the inside out. This time do not step out but see the same council member as a second picture in front of you, this time even bigger and brighter.

7. Now step forward into the bigger and brighter council member, and notice these good feelings double.

8. Now see another picture in front of you of the same council member. This time when you step forward into this image, the feelings will double again. Step forward and experience feeling even better!

9. Once again, see another picture of your council member in front of you even bigger and brighter and step in, doubling these amazing feelings again.

You can practice this skill numerous times until it becomes so natural to step into the image of a council member and experience the qualities and abilities that you wish to emulate. And, of course, if you wish to double and triple these feelings, we can't stop you!

We do suggest, however, that you go through the New Behavior Generator with only one of your advisers per session. To do this pattern with more than one council member would be somewhat overwhelming and could "muddy the waters." Your neurology needs the time to fully embody and become familiar with each adviser individually. So we recommend giving yourself plenty of time between sessions.

Chapter 12: The BEAT Pattern

The BEAT Pattern (created by Shawn Carson and based on the work of John Overdurf's *Mind Power for Life*) works on the approach of anchoring states. We are aware that a state is more than simply an emotion or a feeling. A state includes these plus our awareness, our physiology, and our thoughts. The BEAT Pattern focuses on integrating all of these aspects and anchoring them so that it can be easily used. In this chapter, we discuss what the BEAT Pattern is and how it can be used and applied to the CIA.

One aspect of the BEAT Pattern that makes it unique is that you get to "walk in the shoes of another person." You see, the BEAT Pattern utilizes spatial anchors. This means that you will physically move from space to space taking on the different characteristics of another. In this case, it is likely that you will be taking on the characteristics of one of your advisers.

Within this pattern, you will not only be walking in the steps of one of your council members but also taking on some of her physical gestures too. The motor cortex of the brain is activated by physical movement, observing movement, or simply imagining physical movement. This pattern utilizes all three: observing, imagining, and moving. These gestures, movements, and physiology are all done within a light trance. This allows the mind to unconsciously practice any skills before taking these characteristics into the conscious or outside world.

The BEAT Pattern is an acronym for the following:

B = Body/breathing
E = Emotions
A = Attention/awareness
T = Thoughts

The BEAT Pattern also uses three types of anchors. An anchor is a basic stimulus/response mechanism. You probably have a number of anchors already in your life. Have you ever had the experience of hearing a song and it immediately reminding you of another time and place? Or maybe you smell cookies baking somewhere and are immediately transported to a memory of baking cookies with your grandmother. Maybe you feel a certain emotion, possibly pride, when you see your flag being raised at the Olympic. Or you find that your foot has immediately moved to the break pedal the moment you see a red traffic light. These are all anchors. You experience a stimulus (the smell of cookies) and experience an immediate response (memory of baking with Grandma).

Anchors are found in all of our sensory systems. They can also be spatial. We become used to certain areas around us being used for specific tasks, and these may evoke certain emotions and states. You probably go into work mode when you open your computer or step into your office, and have a different set of emotions on opening your front door at the end of the day.

These are examples of spatial anchors where the physical space itself evokes a specific state or emotion. These emotions have been set unconsciously; in fact, they just seem to happen. In change work, we can set anchors intentionally that are then used as positive resources for the client or for ourselves.

The BEAT Pattern uses four types of anchors that are set intentionally:

1. Spatial
2. Kinesthetic
3. Auditory
4. Visual

The CIA for the BEAT includes a visual anchor. Although this can be included in the regular BEAT, it *has* to be included here, as you or your client will be making a picture of the adviser on each steppingstone, and this acts as a visual anchor.

Basic Steps of the BEAT for CIA

The BEAT Pattern takes the New Behavior Generator one step further; in fact, it takes it three steps further!

As mentioned before, this is a spatial pattern, so we begin by asking the client, or yourself, to imagine four areas in the space, each one representing one letter of the B–E–A–T.

Each space is like its own steppingstone in the pathway, and on each space, we focus on one aspect of the council member. Each space will also have its own spatial anchor (the physical space), kinesthetic anchor (squeezing together the thumb and a certain finger), auditory anchor (saying the letter), and visual anchor (seeing the image of the adviser).

Step 1:

On the first steppingstone, you see your chosen adviser slightly larger than life size. Notice her posture, breathing, facial expression, gestures, and any physical attributes. When you are ready, step forward into the role model. Now anchor the changes in physiology using a visual, kinesthetic, auditory, and spatial anchor. The visual anchor is the image of the council member. The spatial anchor is represented by the space on the floor. The kinesthetic anchor is to squeeze together the thumb and forefinger together. And the auditory anchor is to say the letter *B*.

Step 2:

Here you check in with your emotional state. Is your emotional state the same as you imagine your council member's when he is engaging in the behavior? It is likely that it will be because you have just stepped into his physiology, and his physiology reflects his state. If it isn't the same (as you imagine) your council member's to be, then this step gives you the chance to change states. You can do this by asking yourself, "Are my values the same as my council member's? And if so, when I get in touch with those values, when I am living them, where do I feel that in my body?" If your values are not aligned with those of your council member's, you will likely not be able to match his emotional state, although this does not mean he can't be in your council.

Step 3:

On the third steppingstone, you check in with your attention and awareness, both how you are paying attention and what you are paying attention to. Are you paying attention to the world around you in the way that you imagine your council member is? By this, we mean using your senses—your eyes, ears, nose, and your sense of touch, balance, and movement. Are you paying attention to the things that you believe your chosen council member pays attention to, and are you paying attention in the same way you imagine she would? Are you in peripheral vision (a wide, open "taking it all in" vision) or foveal vision (specifically focused vision) or split attention (a mixture of moving between the two styles)? If not, this step gives you the opportunity to recalibrate your sensory awareness of the imaginary world around you.

Step 4:

On the fourth step, you check in with your thoughts. Are you thinking the thoughts you imagine your council member is thinking when he engaged in the behavior? Are you believing the same things about yourself and your own capabilities as he does? Do you and your council member have the same thoughts and beliefs about the world and the people around you? If not, this step gives you the option to recalibrate your thoughts about the world around you.

The BEAT Pattern for CIA in Practice

> Coach: I know you have lots of wonderful members on your council. Who would you like to do this pattern with today?

> Client: I would like to do this process with Helen of Troy.

> Coach: Great. And is there one particular aspect of Helen of Troy you are interested in?

> Client: Yes, her confidence.

> Coach: OK. And is there a time and a place in your life where you would like to feel more confident?

> Client: Yes, particularly during sales meetings.

> Coach: OK, that's fantastic. OK, so now I would like you to begin by imagining four spaces, or steppingstones, in a line in front of you. Each space will represent a different letter of the BEAT Pattern, B–E–A–T.

(Client nods.)

Coach: Now I would like you to bring to mind four Helens of Troy. Each one is standing on one of the steppingstones. So you have a Helen of Troy on the *B*, a Helen only the *E*, one on the *A* steppingstone, and the last Helen of Troy is standing on the *T* steppingstone. Now, as you look at the first Helen of Troy standing on the *B* steppingstone, I want you to focus particularly on her body and on her physiology. How is she holding herself? What is her face facial expression? Look at everything. Become aware of her rate of breathing. Does she breathe high or from her belly or somewhere in between? And when you have as clear a representation as possible, I would like you to go ahead and step into the Helen on the *B* steppingstone and take on all of these physical attributes, holding your body in the same way, breathing in the same way.

(Coach observes that the client is shifting her physiology while observing the Helen of Troy even before she steps in. Client steps forward and takes on the physiology even more.)

Coach: Right. Now I would like you to pinch together your thumb and index finger and say the letter *B*.

(Client does so.)

Coach: Great. Now I would like you to step aside from the steppingstones and take a look at the Helen of Troy who is standing on the *E* steppingstone. For this Helen of Troy, I would like you to focus on the emotions she is experiencing, particularly her confidence. How do you know she's confident? What is it about her that is letting you know that she is a confident young woman? When you are ready, go ahead and step into the Helen of Troy on the E steppingstone.

(Coach observes the client shifting, and then the client does so.)

Coach: And where are you feeling this confidence in your body?

Client: I can feel it in my chest.

Coach: Does it have a size or a shape or a color?

Client: Yes, it feels like she is wearing armor on the inside. It's shiny and silver.

Coach: Fantastic! Now I would like you to pinch together your thumb and middle finger while saying the letter E.

(Client does so.)

Coach: Now step aside from the steppingstones, come stand next to me, and take a look at the Helen of Troy who is standing on the A steppingstone. What I would like you to notice here is where her attention is. What is she focusing on? How is she focusing? Is she in a wide peripheral vision? Or is her attention focused? What is it that you believe she is focusing on?

Client: I'm not sure, but I can sense something.

Coach: OK. Go ahead and step into the Helen of Troy on the *A* steppingstone and notice what you notice.

(Client steps forward.)

Coach: What's happening now?

Client: There is an expansiveness to her awareness; it is as though I can see everything.

Coach: Is there something in particular you are focusing on?

Client: I am focusing on everything that is outside of myself.

Coach: Great. Now I would like you to squeeze together your thumb and ring finger while saying the letter *A*.

(Client does so.)

Coach: Great. Step aside from this steppingstone, come stand next to me, and take a look at the final Helen of Troy. She is standing on the *T* steppingstone. In this position, what do you believe her thoughts to be?

Client: At the moment, I don't think there are many thoughts.

Coach: OK. Would it help if you step into this position? Maybe you will have more understanding, a different experience when you stand on the *T* steppingstone.

Client: OK.

(Client moves into the T steppingstone position.)

Client: I'm still not sure.

Coach: OK. Would it help to imagine that you, as Helen of Troy, are about to meet somebody whom you wish to persuade or positively influence?

Client: Oh, that's different. Now I am saying to myself, "I can do this."

Coach: Fantastic! Now squeeze together your thumb and pinky while saying the letter T.

(Client does this.)

Coach: Step off the steppingstone and come and stand next to me.

(Client moves and stands next to the coach.)
Coach: Now you have the four steppingstones lined up. I want you to start again at the B steppingstone and step into the physiology while squeezing together your thumb and index finger for a few moments. Then, when you are ready, step forward into the A position pressing together your thumb and middle finger, then the E position, and finally the T position firing the anchors on your fingers for each steppingstone. Take as much time as you would like in each position until you fully embody each aspect. Remember, when you have finished with the final steppingstone, step away from the pathway to make your return to the beginning.

(Client takes a few moments to go through this process.)

Coach: How was that?

Client: Fantastic!

Coach: Great. Let's do it again to really consolidate it; in fact, let's do it a few more times.

Client: Great.

Coach: Each time, though, I want you to get faster and faster so eventually you are just stepping from one steppingstone to the next whilst firing those anchors on your fingers.

(Client does this five more times getting faster each time.)

Coach: How is it now?

Client: This is wonderful.

Coach: Now I would like you to simply stand here and fire the four anchors, one on each finger, and notice what happens.

(Client does so. Coach observes the physiological shifts in the client.)

Client: Oh, wow, that's amazing!

Coach: And now I would like you to think of going into your next sales meeting, and as you do, fire off these quick and simple anchors and notice how it is different now.

(Client does so.)

Client: Oh, this feels so different.

Coach: Fantastic! Now I would like you to think of a few more times in the future when you will be having sales meetings and would like this level of confidence or even more! And you find that each one can become easier as your confidence expands and develops, so much so that you don't even need to fire those anchors on your fingers. Your confidence is just right there whenever you need it!

(Client spends a few moments imagining sales meetings in the future. Coach notices the change in physiology.)

Additional Comments

We can think of the first time through the pattern as a setup phase. The coach asks the client to step into the steppingstone, experience the particular aspect, and then come and stand next to her before stepping into the next steppingstone. Because the client is experiencing the attribute for the first time, and the specific anchors are being set, it is important to allow the neurology to establish the correct neural network associated with the specific attribute. This needs to be done in a very clear manner. Asking the client to step in, experience and set the anchor, and then step out allows her to reset between each experience. Once the four aspects have been established, the coach asks the client to step from one stone to another, each time taking enough time to embody the breathing, emotions, awareness, and thoughts and firing off the anchors. You can think of this as the second phase where these attributes become linked. You will also be aware that client was asked to step off the T steppingstone before returning to the start position. It is important to ensure that your client does not simply walk backwards or turn around and walk backwards through the steppingstones.

You may also have noticed that the coach observed the client taking on the physicality or physiology before stepping into the image in the steppingstone. We know that the body is the first thing that shows us that change is taking place, and we do not ask the client to step into the image until we have seen that she is already beginning to take on the specific aspect

The coach also tied this particular BEAT into a specific context for the client. It is simply not enough to make our clients feel wonderful; we need to attach this particular resource to an area of their life, to a very specific context, where it will be useful for them. In coaching, this is often in an area where the client is experiencing some difficulty or challenge. In the above example, the client was feeling a lack of confidence in sales meetings. Attaching the confidence that was built during the pattern to a specific time and place will help to collapse that negative feeling. If you remember Meta Pattern, this is the fourth step of the Meta Pattern known as *the collapse*. (See our book *The Meta Pattern: The Ultimate Structure for Change*, Shawn and Sarah Carson, 2014.)

The coach also asked the client to imagine five or six future times where she could use this new confidence. Future pacing is an important part of any client work. You may have noticed that the coach suggested that each time the client imagined another future context, her confidence was even more readily available, eventually letting go of the need to pinch the fingers together to fire the anchors. The hope here is that the state becomes automatic and does not need the external trigger.

The Multiperson BEAT Pattern

Another way to use the BEAT Pattern with your CIA is to focus on four members of your cabinet and select one attribute for each that ties in with the BEAT. For example: Instead of asking your client to see four Helens of Troy, you would ask her to see a different member on each steppingstone, each representing a different characteristic.

This might look something like this:

B = Helen of Troy (body/breathing)
E = Coco Chanel (emotions)
A = Thomas Edison (awareness/attention)
T = Martin Luther King, Jr. (thoughts)

You would then ask your client to look at the physiology of Helen of Troy, her body and breathing, step in an take on the physiology and breathing, and then anchor in the same way as before by squeezing together the thumb and index finger and saying B. Stepping away from the steppingstones, you would ask your client to then observe Coco Chanel and what her emotions might be. The process of stepping in and anchoring would be repeated as before. From here, you would ask your client to look at Thomas Edison and his awareness, step in and anchor on the ring finger, and finally consider what thoughts Martin Luther King, Jr., might be experiencing and stepping in and anchoring.

The pattern would then continue as above, asking your client to move through the steppingstones and firing the anchors a few times and then attaching this results into a future experience of context.

This pattern offers a wide variety of options and variations. Many CIAs have six or more members, and each member can be in a different position and with a different combination.

Chapter 13: Tree of Life

We have discussed several times that the more you know about your council members, the deeper and more profound the CIA experiences will be.

To understand your advisers better, you will need to know and understand how they behave, including how they walk, stand, and sit; how they react to events around them; the things they say; their typical feelings and emotional states; what they believe about themselves and the world around them; and their values and what is important to them.

The methods you can use for discovering this information depend upon who the council member is and his relationship to you. For example: If the adviser is someone you actually know (perhaps a family member), you can observe him as he goes about his day. Or sit with him over a coffee or beer and ask him about his life experiences. If the adviser is a person you do not personally know, but is alive (or only recently deceased), there will likely be videos of him on YouTube discussing his life or accomplishments; watching these videos will give you a lot of information about your adviser.

Of course, your adviser may be long dead. For example: I (Shawn) have Hannibal (the famous Carthagian general who led his elephants across the Alps to challenge the might of Rome, not the fictional cannibal!) on my council for his decisive and creative problem solving. Obviously, there are no video interviews of Hannibal on YouTube, no photographs, no audio recordings. However, there is plenty of historical information about his campaigns and several great biographies that I have read.

So whoever you choose to be on your council, you can rest assured that there will be plenty of material for you to watch, listen to, or read to gain a deep understanding of each of your selected advisers.

In this chapter, we show you a great method for organizing the material your find on your adviser to gain a deep and profound understanding of the person's character. This method is based on the Tree of Life from the Kabbalah. (You can discover how to use the Tree of Life in a coaching context by reading *Tree of Life Coaching* by Shawn Carson.)

The Tree of Life provides a model to understand the entirety of human experience in a relatively simple way, through 10 inter-related points of experience:

1. The real or physical world: What are the adviser's physical presence and physical surroundings?

2. The model of the world: What events in the outside world cause the adviser to react? How does the adviser behave to influence the world around her? Essentially, what causes–effects are there where the adviser is either an effect (reacting) or cause (making the world react to her)?

3. Thoughts: What sort of thoughts does the adviser have?

4. Emotions: What emotions does the adviser habitually feel?

5. Beliefs: What beliefs does the adviser hold about herself and her relationship to the world?

6. Values: What values are ultimately important to the adviser?

7. The true unconscious: How does the adviser's unconscious mind combine all the above and reconcile inner conflicts?

8. Archetypal models: Who or what are the important teachers and advisers who made the adviser who she is?

9. Distinctions: What are the important distinctions that the adviser makes when living in her world?

10. The ultimate value: What is the adviser's ultimate value? Perhaps this is her relationship to God or the divine.

When you continuously ask yourself these questions regarding your council member, as you watch, listen to, or read information about her, you will be able to construct a very powerful avatar of her. This avatar will add real value to your CIA.

To clarify how this might work, I (Shawn) will take my adviser Hannibal Barca of Carthage as an example. Hannibal is long dead, but some sculptures exist that are believed to be of him. Looking at these, we see sturdy bearded features of the North African Hannibal. He has been described as having a "bright look" and "fire in his eyes." He was trained to be a warrior from birth, and his contemporaries point out that in spite of leading what was essentially a mercenary army, never had his troops revolted. This was because he never asked his soldiers to do anything that he himself would not do. From this, I see him as a fiery warrior, physically strong and agile.

Hannibal was not known for being a brilliant general. Rather than fighting the Romans in Spain, where he was based, he marched his army into Italy where he faced numerous Roman armies; each led by very capable Roman generals. Yet in every battle, it is Hannibal who chooses the time and place of battle. He is the ultimate person at cause, everyone else reacting to his actions. Indeed, Hannibal is noted as having said, "I will find a way or make one."

While we cannot know for certain what thoughts passed through Hannibal's mind, several of his quotations survive. The most telling for me is the one discussed above, "I will find a way or make one." It seems to me that he is always thinking of what action he can take to conform the world to his will.

As the consummate warrior and general, Hannibal did not openly show softer emotions. One of his famous quotes is, "God has given to man no sharper spur to victory than contempt of death." In my council, Hannibal appears as a fearless, if somewhat reserved or even taciturn, man of action. Hannibal has complete belief in himself.

Hannibal was ultimately defeated by the Roman general Scipio Africanus. When they met some years later, Scipio, no doubt fishing for a compliment, asked Hannibal who he considered the greatest general of all time, to which Hannibal replied Alexander the Great. Scipio asked Hannibal for his second choice, and Hannibal choose another contemporary general, Pyrrhus. Scipio pressed Hannibal for his third choice, to which Hannibal said himself, Hannibal. Frustrated, Scipio asked where Hannibal would rank himself had Scipio not beaten him, to which Hannibal said in that case he would rank himself above Alexander. This exchange demonstrates why Hannibal shows complete belief in himself on my council!

Hannibal lived according to several key values—these emerge strongly from reading his biographies. Absolute courage in the face of death and equality in sharing the hardships of his soldiers are two that I mentioned above, but perhaps even more important was his complete loyalty to Carthage. Even though as a child he swore eternal enmity to Rome, after the defeat of Carthage, Hannibal took over the running of Carthage from incompetent leaders who had betrayed him, in part to pay the penalties that Rome had imposed.

Hannibal appears to me as a completely integrated individual. Once he has decided on a goal or outcome agreed in my council, Hannibal shows a single-minded focus on bringing this to pass. As in his own life, there are no half measures, no uncertainty, no doubts.

Hannibal was the son of Hamilcar Barca, one of Carthage's greatest generals, whose name, *Barca,* means "lightning bolt." Hamilcar took the 10-year-old Hannibal with him when he went to conquer Spain on behalf of Carthage, from which time Hannibal lived with the soldiers in military camp while his father campaigned. Hannibal was the ultimate warrior and general in a long line of soldiers. As such, he has a purity of character in my CIA.

Hannibal's distinctions are simple and clear, adding to the clarity of his character. Carthage versus Rome, honor versus death, the possible versus the unattempted. No doubt Hannibal worshipped the gods of Carthage, but his loyalty was to Carthage herself and against everything that Rome stood for.

In summary, everything about Hannibal, and his role on my CIA, is simple and direct. He does not generally question why something should be done, but will always question why it should be done in the way suggested. Present him with a choice of outcomes and he may not have an opinion. But present him with one goal and he will present a direct and imaginative plan for reaching it.

Keeping the Tree of Life model in mind will allow you to build up a rich, complex, and accurate avatar for each of your council members based on the research that you do.

Chapter 14: The Perfect Coach Pattern

Growing up in the UK, I was unfamiliar with the concept of going to summer camp. When I was around 16 years old, I was accepted into a summer school for young artists. This was a two-week program held in a small beautiful village about an hour from my home. I was excited about the prospect of attending and was also aware that this would be the first time I would be away from my family for this long a period. Of course, I had been to stay with other family members or friends for a week or so without my parents, but I was going to a camp where I knew nobody, so it felt like a "first" for me.

I remember my father driving me to camp, and although I was excited and looking forward to the experience, I was also nervous. Was I good enough? Would I fit in? Would the other students and teachers be nice and friendly? I had many questions and was probably playing some less than useful movies in my mind as to how the experience could possibly turn out. I remember talking to my father on the journey and letting him know that I was a bit scared.

My father listened to me patiently and gave me kindly words of encouragement and support. My father was an art teacher, and I had spent my life being coached and taught by him in painting and drawing. At one point he said, "And if you just take a moment and close your eyes and think about how I would advise you, then it will be as though I am right there with you." I immediately relaxed. I realized that everything would be OK because I had this as an inner resource: not only a loving father who could guide me and support me through personal issues but also a skilled teacher who could advise and suggest ideas.

Take a moment now and consider how fantastic it would be to have your own personal coach at your side, at any time and for any given situation. Maybe you can bring to mind a situation where this would have been useful for you. Imagine for a moment having Tony Robbins by your side to inspire or motivate you, or perhaps Leonardo da Vinci by your side for a creative project.

The Perfect Coach Pattern provides exactly this experience. You can use it to give a coach more skills from an even more experienced and knowledgeable coach, and to teach a client how to become even more resilient. As a hypnotist or coach, you can lead your clients through this pattern so that they always have the perfect coach by their side for any situation.

This pattern can be adapted for use with the CIA Pattern. It is possible to select one of your council members who would be the most appropriate perfect coach for a specific situation. When someone is experiencing an issue or a problem, it is as though the person is stuck in the problem. We have probably all experienced a moment of having an issue and struggling to find a positive outcome or result. This is because we view every possibility through the lens of a problem. In other words, it is as though we wear spectacles labeled "problem," and this negatively colors any options, suggestions, or alternatives that we see. The Perfect Coach Pattern allows us to easily dissociate from ourselves—and, consequently, from the problem—and associate into a position where we have full access to all the available resources.

The pattern is as follows:

- Go into trance and associate into a specific time and place where you are experiencing your issue or problem. Be very specific. For example: If you are have a problem with public speaking, select one time when you have experienced this. Associate into it and see what you are seeing, hear what you are hearing, and feel what you are feeling.

- Invite your selected council member to join you in this space.

- Ask your selected member for permission to step inside of him for coaching. Be sure to make the purpose of this process very clear to your council member.

- Now, as a consciousness, float out of yourself and into a fly-on-the wall position. From this position, you should be able to see the "you" and your council member. From this dissociated position, notice the physiology, breathing, and posture of your council member. You will also see the physiology of the "you" down there. Take on or mirror the physiology of your council member.

- When you are ready, float into your council member. Take a few moments to adjust and orient yourself, continuing to be aware of your breathing and posture and noticing what it is like to see through these eyes and hear through these ears. Become aware of your emotions and how you feel as this person. Notice everything you are aware of as your council member. What are you believing about yourself? What are you believing about the world as this person? What is of value to you? What is important to you?

- Now, as your council member, observe the "you" in this

specific context. See, with the eyes of your council member, the behaviors and emotions that the real you is experiencing and expressing. What are you aware of as your council member about the "you" in this particular situation?

As this totally resourceful council member, you can begin to help the "you" to change his thoughts, behaviors, emotions, and feelings. As this council member, guide, lead, support, and advise the "you" to becoming more resourceful. As the council member, observe how the "you" is changing. Notice changes in physiology that will let you know that the "you" has changed in a positive resourceful and beneficial manner.

Once this change and shift has taken place, you can go to another time and place when the "you" experienced the same problem and coach him once again. Repeat this as many times as necessary based on what feels right.

Now you can take a moment to become your own best future coach. There will be a time in the future that the "you" may need a best coach. And you, as the council member, can be there waiting to guide him through the situation. Indeed, there may be numerous times and places in the future when the "you" could use the guidance and support of this council member. Practice now imagining future contexts and running through each of these guiding and supporting the "you" to become the best the real you can be.

When you are ready, return to the first context and step outside of the council member and back into the fly-on-the-wall position. Now float back into yourself and notice how things are different. Take a moment to thank your council member for the wonderful coaching and guidance he has given you.

As your council member already knows, there may be times in the future when you could use your council members' support and guidance. As yourself, go to one of those times in the future now and experience receiving coaching. Your council members know exactly how to make this different for you so that you feel confident in your resilience.

Once you have finished, you can return fully and completely to the here and now.

Chapter 15: NLP Disney Pattern

The Disney Pattern is an NLP pattern that allows us to sequentially associate into three different archetypes. Although the NLP Disney Pattern does not necessarily require these archetypes to be personified as real people, as in the council, they have the attributes of creativity, skepticism, and practicality. The names of these three archetypes are the Dreamer, the Critic, and the Realist. The Disney Pattern allows the client to move from being associated into the Dreamer and then to associate into the Critic (or sometimes the Realist), followed by the Realist (respectively, Critic).

The association into the Dreamer, Critic, and Realist typically takes place using spatial anchors. In fact, Walt Disney was said to go through this pattern using three different rooms, one assigned to each of the archetypes. The pattern also relies on different physiologies to create the appropriate states for each Dreamer, Critic, and Realist.

We will use the principles of the Disney Pattern to create a working group within your council of advisers. For this pattern to work using your council members, you need to set the spatial anchors and characteristics of your chosen members before posing any questions or raising any issues to discuss.

You can run the CIA version of the Disney Pattern in one of

two ways. The first and simplest way is to form a working group of the three council members you have selected to represent the Dreamer, Critic, and Realist. The second way is to use the New Behavior Generator or the BEAT Pattern to actually associate into each of the three advisers in turn.

We outline the first approach using an example from my (Shawn's) council. (You can find a description of Shawn's full CIA in Appendix 2.)

For this exercise, I chose the following three council members for the Dreamer, Critic, and Realist archetypes in the Disney Pattern.

1. Dreamer, Leonardo da Vinci: Leonardo is the consummate dreamer, and possibly the most pure archetype from history for this role. After all, Leonardo dreamed into existence the concept of the helicopter, parachute, and scuba diving gear centuries before the world had the engineering skills to make them a reality.

2. Critic, Richard Feynman: Professor Feynman was an amazingly creative mind in his own right, and could easily serve the role of the Dreamer. However, his role in analyzing the *Challenger* space shuttle disaster convinced me of his ability to critically analyze complex issues and discover actual or potential faults that could derail an otherwise great idea.

3. Realist, Hannibal Barca of Carthage: Having been instructed by Carthage to do the impossible—defeat the mighty Roman Empire—Hannibal set out to invade Italy, defeat every Roman army sent against him, and bring Rome to her knees. Only his lack of siege equipment to overcome Rome's defenses prevented him from achieving ultimate victory.

I (Shawn) used this process when I was suffering work overload. I had a number of different projects, each with its own deadlines. Trying to manage the expectations of each stakeholder in each project was leading to a great deal of stress. I arranged to meet with my three archetypes—Leonardo, Feynman, and Hannibal—in turn.

I met with Leonardo first and found myself in a room inside a magnificent Renaissance building with a massive domed ceiling. In the middle of the floor, Leonardo sat in front of a canvas, painting. I moved closer and saw he was painting a mechanical knight or robot (this was actually one of Leonardo's inventions). As I continued to watch, the painting began to complete itself with many more of these fabulous robots appearing as I drifted off to sleep.

Upon wakening, I realized the meaning of Leonardo's visual communication was to use the other people involved in each project more effectively. Immediately, my inner critic leapt to the attack, although not in the expected form of Professor Feynman, but rather a disembodied voice that raised all sorts of objections. I decided to return to the issue the next night to see if these objections could be overcome by the Realist.

Much to my surprise, upon starting my day's tasks, I found myself seized by a driving determination—or should I say by the spirit of Hannibal Barca? I spent the morning visiting or calling other stakeholders in each project and forcefully discussing with them what I needed them to do. By the end of the day, I found that much of my backlogged to-do list had disappeared (or perhaps reappeared on someone else's list).

Using Association in the CIA Disney Pattern

In the traditional Disney Pattern, you would seek to develop (via the Dreamer) a solution to your issue, discover any potential weak points in that solution (via the Critic), and address those weak points (via the Realist). For each step in the process, you would personally step into the role of Dreamer then Critic then Realist.

You can follow this process in the CIA Disney Pattern simply by stepping into each of your chosen council members rather than meeting with them. You can do this using the NLP New Behavior Generator or the BEAT Pattern (using one council member at a time).

Remember, with the New Behavior Generator and the BEAT Pattern, it is important that you have physiological shifts when moving from one state to another, or when moving from being associated into one council member to being associated into another council member. It is, therefore, important to consider and note the physiological patterns of each council member so that she can be adopted when associating into that member. What is her posture like? What is her breathing like? What is her facial expression? What are her gestures? How does she move?

Part 1: Setup for the Disney Pattern with CIA

- Select three members of the Council of Advisers, one to represent each characteristic of the Dreamer, the Critic, and the Realist.

- Using the New Behavior Generator or the BEAT Pattern, associate into each selected council member. Do this in different chairs or specific places in the room to anchor the experience.

Part 2: Disney CIA Pattern

- Select an issue to work through.

- Sit in the Dreamer chair/space and give the perspective from this position. Remember to dream big. Come up with the grandest plans and biggest ideas possible!

- Move to the Critic chair and give perspective on the issue from this point of view. Remember, this position is not one of nastiness, but one of pointing out the flaws and errors, providing constructive criticism, and looking for holes in the plan.

- Move to the third chair, the Realist position, and give the perspective on the issue from this point of view. Here you can come up with solutions, alternatives, and possible answers.

- Move back and forth between the chairs as you feel is most appropriate to have an exchange of ideas on the issue.

- When you are finished, write down your observations on the process.

Chapter 16: The Polar Sphinx Pattern

Have you ever had a choice to make, where you can see the pros and cons of either side, but you're still not sure which is better? Or perhaps been in a situation where you can argue for one side of an issue and then say, "But on the other hand"? Or maybe you have had the experience of having two options that both seem great but you have to choose only one. This is a fairly common experience and one that most of us will have encountered at some point in our lives.

If you come across a situation similar, you can ask your counsel for advice and use the Polar Sphinx Pattern to help generate a solution. The Polar Sphinx Pattern takes two members of your council with opposing views and asks them to express their particular viewpoints and then seeks resolution by asking the members to change perspective.

The Polar Sphinx Pattern is so called because it offers the polar opposite arguments and is resolved (or given an alternative perspective) from the Sphinx. In classical mythology, the Sphinx was the gatekeeper to the ancient city of Thebes. To be granted entry, one had to answer this riddle posed by the Sphinx: "What walks on four legs in the morning, two legs and noon, and three legs in the evening?" Oedipus solved the riddle and was given access to the city. The Sphinx also posed a second riddle: "There are two sisters: one gives birth to the other and she, in turn, gives birth to the first. Who are the two sisters?" The answer is day and night. It is this use of opposites that gives us the name used in this pattern. You can think of the two sides of your argument as thesis and antithesis and the Sphinx acting as the resolution or synthesis.

This pattern is based on the traditional NLP pattern called the Visual Squash. Here we find both sides of the argument or dilemma, tease out the respective values for each side, give these ideas from one side to the other, and eventually find common ground either in a shared value or in a value that has the same energy surrounding it.

The Polar Sphinx Pattern does a similar thing by selecting two council members with opposing views, asking both for their opinions and what is important to them, and then asking them to switch seats. The final answer or resolution may then come to the chairperson in trance or through sleep incubation.

Here is how the Polar Sphinx Pattern works.

Think of a context or situation where you may be experiencing a dilemma or a decision. This may be new to you, or it can be something that you have already discussed with your council.

Go into trance and take yourself to your meeting place. Ask your council members to appear. Note where everyone sits. It is likely that your council members take the same seats each time they meet and, as such, have become anchored to their seating positions. This will become more important in the Sphinx portion of this pattern.

Choose the two council members you believe have the most opposing views on this issue, and ask them if they are willing to participate in this meeting. If they agree, ask these two to stay and your other council members to leave. If one or both are not agreeable, select another member.

Explain your issue, question, or dilemma to your two council members. Tell them that you would like them to state their point of view, putting forth their position one at a time. Choose one member to go first. When that member has finished, invite the other member to speak. Make sure they are still sitting in the same chairs in which they usually sit, or standing in the same position where they usually stand.

Having heard the point of view from each of the two members, ask them to switch seats. Watch as they stand from their seats and walk around to sit in each other's position. Now ask them again one by one how they feel about the issue. And notice what happens.

Here is an extract from my CIA work.

> I explained to the council that I am uncertain whether to keep the Polar Sphinx Pattern as its own individual chapter or include it in the "Interacting with Your Council" chapter. I asked if any of the council members have strong opinions about this.
>
> Eleanor Roosevelt said, "Yes, I think it should be its own, a standalone chapter."
>
> Steve Jobs immediately jumped in and said, "Well, I'm not so sure. I think it should be part of the 'Interacting with Your Council' chapter."
>
> My two council members for the Polar Sphinx Pattern have self-selected, and I thanked them and asked if they were willing to work with me on this pattern. They both agreed, and I asked the other members of my council to leave. The

other members of the council simply faded, leaving Eleanor, Steve, and me in the white pavilion.

I asked Eleanor and Steve to remain seated in their usual places, and I sat in my usual space. I explained that I would ask each person to put forward his or her point of view, without interruption.

Eleanor spoke first and said, "I think the Polar Sphinx Pattern should be its own individual chapter. It is a clear pattern for solving issues and dilemmas and deserves a full chapter. You are using this specific pattern to help you write the book and will undoubtedly include a transcript of this very meeting."

I turned to Steve and he said, "Well, I think we have to consider the difference between the 'Interacting with Your Council' chapter and the chapters that explain individual patterns. It seems to me that the exercises and suggestions included in the 'Interacting your Council' chapter offer suggestions of how to interact with your council members at different times while the individual chapters are opportunities to step inside each individual council member to get to know them more deeply. These individual chapters also lay out how to utilize the changes in a more traditional hypnotic or NLP sense. I think this particular pattern is more about the interaction with the council as opposed to a traditional NLP pattern."

I thanked them both for their respective points of view, and we moved into the Sphinx part of this pattern.

I asked Eleanor Roosevelt and Steve Jobs to then stand up and to switch places. I watched as Eleanor walked around the chairs to sit in Steve's chair and Steve walked to sit in the chair where Eleanor usually sits.

As soon as Eleanor Roosevelt sat down in Steve Jobs chair, I noticed a shift in her physiology. Her head tilted to one side, and she looked very thoughtful for a moment. I asked her how she felt, and she responded that although she still felt that the pattern deserved its own chapter, she could see that it also could have a place in the "Interacting with Your Council" chapter. It really could be in either or both.

I turned to Steve Jobs and asked what he felt. He replied that he still felt that it should be included in the "Interacting with Your Council" chapter because he didn't see that it was as NLP-like a pattern as the New Behavior Generator, the BEAT Pattern, or the Perfect Coach Pattern.

I asked him if he felt it offered more insight into the council members, and he said, "Yes, to a point. The other patterns ask the client to step into the council members, and this one was purely observational."

I could see just how focused and stubborn Steve Jobs was about this, and that gave me more insight into his character!

I thanked both Eleanor and Steve for joining me in this process and offering me even more insight and perspective.

Even though this particular interaction did not offer me the answer or solution. It did give me more to think about and helped me in making my final decision.

If there is no clear resolution, and you want to take the process further, feel free to explore the following additional steps:

1. Repeat the process a couple of times. Have each council member return to his own chair and restate his position incorporating the information he obtained by sitting in the other council member's chair.

2. Have both advisers swap chairs and, rather than asking them simply how they feel, ask them what they feel is important to their colleague, from the perspective of sitting in his chair. Once they have identified one or more values that their colleague has, reflected in their colleague's position, have them return to their own chair and come up with a new proposal that incorporates both their values and those of their colleague.

Conclusion: Other Ways to Use Your CIA

We have offered numerous methods for creating your council, explained how to establish a meeting space, given ideas of how to interact with your CIA, and explained the importance of dream incubation. We have shared numerous NLP patterns and explained how these underlie the principles involved in the CIA and how the two can be used in conjunction.

Now it is time for you to go out and, if you haven't done so already, create your own Council of Inner Advisers.

We will leave you with a few more ideas of different styles of councils. Of course, this list is not exhaustive, and I am pretty sure that you will come up with more ideas and suggestions than just these.

Now go play and have fun!

Anti-Council

As New Yorkers, we often use lessons learned from the TV show *Seinfeld* to inform our change work. In one episode, George Costanza decides that everything he has ever done in his life is a disaster, so he should start doing the opposite of whatever his instinct tells him. Needless to say, his life is transformed for the better.

In this variation of the CIA, you will form an anti-council, made up of anyone or everyone you would not take advice from, ever!

This may sound very counterintuitive; however, by doing so, this anti-council may represent various aspects of how you are now when you are in your problem issue. This could offer a great deal of insight to you regarding how your problem arises. By essentially doing the opposite of what this anti-council suggests, you may find yourself moving in the right direction.

The anti-council process can also act as something of a compulsion blowout, where you become tired of hearing the same excuses and are, therefore, compelled to change. Of course, you may wish to have a further council made up of those from whom you would take advice.

Military Council

This is a council for strategic thinking, made up of the greatest military minds of history. You may wish to include someone in charge "on the ground," a detail oriented planner, a negotiator, a coordinator, maybe a maverick strategic thinker, a leader of men, and a fierce warrior to "lead the troops."

Super Villain Council

You may be thinking that a Council of Inner Advisers made up of super villains would have a very negative or potentially evil focus. However, when you stop to think about it, super villains are a most intriguing group of people (or creatures!) and could be a most interesting and powerfully effective CIA.

Super villains work well together and are super creative. Interestingly enough, their plans are nearly always about having a vision (be it to take over the world) and almost never about revenge. You may wish to include on this type of council a good strategizer, an expeditor, a leader, someone who is not afraid to get his hands dirty, a visionary, and a member who can stand between good and evil (like Magneto from *X-Men*).

Spiritual Council

Having a personal relationship with figures from the Christian Bible, particularly the New Testament, has been a part of Christian spirituality at least since St. Ignatius developed his spiritual exercises in the 16th century.

Having a spiritual CIA does not necessarily have to be a religious council—although it very well could be. You may wish to have a council made up of certain people from your particular holy book or faith. Maybe you would like a council that includes gods and goddesses from a variety of faiths. Or perhaps a CIA that includes such roles as a karmic bookkeeper, someone enraptured with nature, a council member to represent being in love with the divine, and a practical caregiver.

Ancestral, Cultural, or Past Lives Council

Imagine a council that included your great-grandmother who lived through the great depression, maybe your Great-uncle Joe who served in the First World War, and your family members who survived an arduous journey to settle in a new homeland. What experiences and traits could you glean from their experiences?

Or maybe you could fill your CIA with your past life personas if you are fortunate enough to have experienced these. Or perhaps you could create a council with advisers taking such roles as cultural historian, family record keeper, tall-story teller (for those family stories you really wish were true!), DNA writer, and others who weave the threads that link your story from generation to generation.

Writers Council

This book was written with the assistance of a personal writers council. No doubt, you have become familiar with the members of my council. However this is not the only form that a writers council could take.

If you are not a writer, maybe you could have a life as a book/movie council with a screenwriter, director, actors, stars, an editor, a publicist, and, of course, a cheering audience!

Body, Mind, and Soul Council

You could create a council to ensure your own health and well-being of your body, mind, and soul. This could include someone to encourage or enhance your faith either in a religious manner or to connect with something greater than yourself, a physical coach or trainer, someone to help you attune to your body—a hypnotist, mental coach, meditation expert, and so on.

Hypnotist Council

If you are a hypnotist, NLPer, or coach, you may wish to explore the idea of having a hypnosis/coaching CIA. This could include well-known hypnotists and coaches from differing schools and approaches. Maybe an Ericksonian, a direct hypnotist, an indirect hypnotist, an EFT specialist, a new age or traditional coach, a Bandler style NLPer, and a Grinder "New Code" NLPer.

Epic Tale Council

This could be a council made up entirely of the characters from a new or classic epic saga. These sagas usually have many different characters to choose from, both good guys and "baddies," and could prove a most interesting CIA.

Imagine a Council of Inner Advisers made up entirely from the characters within *Game of Thrones*, *Lord of the Rings*, Homer's *Odyssey*, *Star Wars*, or *Harry Potter*. Who would you select? Or maybe one council to bind them all?

Appendix One:
Using the CIA Pattern to Write This Book

Introduction

Starting to write a new book, for me, is always an exciting moment. My head is usually filled with lots of exciting ideas. I have a picture of holding the finished book in my mind's eye, and I'm excited and eager to share my ideas with a wider audience. Now, I have written books before, and I am well aware of my own personal journey and experience as a writer. I know that I am highly enthusiastic and excited at the prospect of writing a book and love to take myself to the moment of having my book published and holding it in my hands for the first time. I am also very well aware that there is a great deal of hard work necessary to complete any book.

I know myself very well, and I know that this enthusiasm tends to fade over time. I know I can get lazy and that all too often writing another chapter of my book goes to the bottom of my to-do list. Knowing this about myself, and knowing that this was going to be a book about creating and using the Council of Inner Advisers, it seemed to make perfect sense to me to create my own Council of Inner Advisers specifically to advise and guide me in the writing of this book. What a wonderful opportunity not only to give myself additional support but also to use the very technique I would be sharing with a wider audience to write the book!

In documenting my journey with my CIA for writing I'm also able to share a real-life experience of creating and using a CIA. Within this account of my experience, I hope to clearly outline how I selected my council members, established our meeting space, and used the council for guidance, decision making, motivation, and deeper understanding.

Postscript

This book was written in about a month, certainly record time for me. I had a sharper focus, more drive, and a "just-do-it-ness" and was excited throughout the process.

My journey and personal experience with my CIA is testimony to the powerful effectiveness of this pattern.

Selecting Members for My CIA

I knew that I was about to create a CIA for a very specific purpose: writing a book. The first step in my journey was to take some time to reflect on my previous experiences in writing a book. This was a moment to be brutally honest with myself, become aware of my own strengths and weaknesses, and begin to highlight certain aspects or skills that I felt I could really use in the writing of this book.

I began by making a list of attributes that I would find most beneficial. I sat quietly for a moment, allowed my breathing to regulate, closed my eyes, and took myself into a light trance. I asked my unconscious mind to generate the qualities and attributes that would be most beneficial to me in writing this book. After a few moments, numerous words appeared in my mind, and I brought myself out of trance and wrote them down.

My list included creativity, just-do-it-ness, being in flow, perseverance, timekeeping, prioritizing, fun, getting things done, and experience.

Looking at this list, one particular attribute stood out to me: the quality of *experience*. I have written a few books in the past, so I knew I had some experience. Yet this word had popped into my mind. I just sat with this word for a few moments, contemplating it and wondering why or how I could use this aspect. In just a few moments, I realized that I was looking for the experience of someone who is a professional writer, someone who has devoted his or her life to writing, someone who is famous for being a writer. My jobs have included being a teacher, hypnotist, and change-worker; writing is something that I had never expected to do. As soon as I began to think about someone who is a writer, someone who's written many books, the author Stephen King came to mind. This was very interesting because I have never read any Stephen King novels! I did, however, know that he is a prolific writer, has published many books, and is widely known and admired. I immediately wrote his name down on my list of potential council members.

From there, I went back to my list of attributes and began to tease out the top five or six qualities that I thought would be the most useful for me. My final list:

- Creativity
- Just-do-it-ness
- Sense of humor
- Experience
- Productivity
- Focus

Taking each of these qualities one at a time, I invited my unconscious mind to generate an individual who embodied this particular trait.

This part of the process, for me, was relatively fast. Within a few moments, I already had suggestions for four of the qualities. I have selected Stephen King for experience, Albert Einstein for creativity, Steve Jobs for focus, and Shawn Carson (my husband and coauthor of this book) for productivity.

Unconscious Selection and Dream Incubation

For the next two members of my council, I decided to use a different method of selection than I had for the previous four. I had consciously/unconsciously selected the previous four members of my council. When I thought about the specific traits and characteristics I required, the names came to mind, and I chose them for the council because they seemed a good fit. I was also aware that all the members I had selected, so far, were male, and I wished to have a more balanced council, so I made a conscious decision to find two women to fill the other two positions. I needed someone who is a motivator, someone who had a 'just-do-it' attitude. I also wanted a member who was able to bring humor and fun to the writing process. I sat and thought consciously about the women who may be able to fulfill these roles, but nobody really sprang to mind, so I asked my unconscious mind to generate possible candidates for both positions while I slept.

Whilst in bed, and just before falling asleep, I took myself to my usual relaxation place—a beautiful white marble pavilion—and simply asked my unconscious mind to come up with a few possibilities of women who could fulfill these particular roles. Before I knew it, I had fallen asleep, and whilst I was sleeping, my unconscious mind was working hard. I'm aware of waking lightly a few times during the night, and each time I was thinking about a woman who would be great for one of these roles. When I fully woke the next morning, I had five women who were potential candidates for the role of motivator and one woman, the British comedienne Victoria Wood, to fulfill the role of fun.

I decided to ask my unconscious mind through the use of my pendulum to show me which of the five women would be the best fit. I sat quietly holding my pendulum between my thumb and pointer finger. I asked the pendulum to show me a "yes" signal, "no" signal, and a "maybe" signal. Once these directions had been established, I went through the list of women, one by one, asking my unconscious mind to show me via the pendulum whether they would be a "yes," a "no," or a "maybe."

Queen Elizabeth I was one of my choices, and as I asked whether she would be the right person to fulfill the role of motivator, the pendulum began to swing very clearly in the "no" direction. I thanked my unconscious mind and moved to my second test, Queen Elizabeth II. The pendulum stayed still in its "maybe" position. I thanked my unconscious mind again and moved to the next woman on the list. The next two candidates, Temple Grandin and the little girl from the Disney movie *Brave*, also received a "maybe" signal from my unconscious mind. The last candidate was Eleanor Roosevelt, and I received a strong "yes" signal from my unconscious mind.

At this point, I did a hypnotic interview with each candidate just to double-check. I closed my eyes and took myself to the white pavilion. Sitting on one of the comfortable white sofas, I invited Queen Elizabeth I to come into the pavilion. I stood, curtsied, and welcomed her to the space. I immediately felt that something was off. I realized that we were not equals, that she exuded such royal presence and expected to be so much higher than anybody else that she probably wasn't the best choice for position on the council where everyone is equal and everyone shares. I invited Queen Elizabeth I to sit with me, and for some unusual reason, my unconscious mind kept moving her over to my right and slightly out of my view. Whenever I changed positions so that we were sitting opposite each other, Elizabeth I continued to move to my right and out of my view. I took this as a very strong indication that Queen Elizabeth I was indeed not the right person to fulfill this role on my council. I thanked her for her time and escorted her out of the white pavilion. I wondered whether part of the reason she was moving out of sight and over to my right was that I had asked her into my own unique personal space as opposed to meeting in either a neutral space or a place that she was familiar with.

For my meeting with Queen Elizabeth II, I decide to trust my unconscious mind to select the right place for us to meet. The scene opened into a private office space that I assumed was an office in Buckingham Palace. Queen Elizabeth II was seated behind an ornate desk in a beautifully appointed room. As I approached the desk, I curtsied and immediately began to explain why we were meeting, about the role and function that would be required of her.

Queen Elizabeth II smiled a big smile and said, "Oh, you think I could do that?"

It was such a funny moment to me because it seemed to show a vulnerability that I had not expected from the queen. I smiled and giggled slightly and said, "Of course, you can do this. I would be honored to have you on my council. Is this something you'd be interested in doing?"

Queen Elizabeth II smiled and said, "Well, thank you so very much for thinking of me. I would be delighted to help. However I'm unusually busy at this time."

I thanked her for her time and for her service and wished her a happy 90th birthday.

The next woman I brought to mind was Temple Grandin. I found myself to be somewhere on a cattle ranch with metal fences, wide-open spaces, and cows all around. Temple Grandin was standing in front of me. A tall lady wearing jeans, a checkered shirt, Stetson hat, and boots.

Before I could even say hello and explain what the role was on my council, Temple Grandin said, "Yes, I'll do it. I'd love to help out." Her enthusiasm was somewhat overwhelming, and she continued, "Tell me where to be, tell me what I have to do. I can help you."

I asked her how she was with other people because there would be six other members on the council and the role was to work together as a team.

She said, "Sure, I can work with other people, but sometimes other people can't work with me."

I smiled and thanked her for her time and said maybe we'd work together on a different project. She seemed like a very cool lady.

The fourth person was somewhat of a surprise from my unconscious mind. It was the young girl from the Disney movie *Brave*. I had seen this movie a number of years ago but did not even remember this character's name. When I called her to mind, we were both climbing a cliff face. Her red hair was flowing behind her. She smiled and said, "Hi." I began to explain why I was here and what the role on the council would be.

She immediately said, "I can do this. I can get to the top. Look at me. Watch me."

I soon realized that she was a great motivator, but as such a young person, her main focus of motivation was for herself. I wondered whether she would be a good guide and motivator for me. I quickly concluded that she wasn't quite ready yet. I thanked her for her time, and with a smile and a wave, left her climbing the cliff.

The last lady I invited to interview was the former First Lady Eleanor Roosevelt. As soon as I brought her to mind, we were sitting in a very elegant tearoom. Eleanor Roosevelt was pouring a cup of tea from the bone china teapot. The table in front of us was laden with plates of sandwiches and cakes. She indicated a chair for me to sit down and said, "How can I help you?"

I explained the situation and the role I required, and she said, "Yes, I can do this. I know exactly how to set the mind to motivate you. I can be like a dog with a bone when it comes to getting things done."

I knew immediately that she was absolutely the right candidate for the job, and I invited Eleanor right then and there to join my CIA Council for writing this book.

So now my council was complete:

- Shawn Carson: productivity
- Stephen King: experience
- Albert Einstein: creativity
- Steve Jobs: focus
- Eleanor Roosevelt: motivation and just-do-it-ness
- Victoria Wood: sense of humor

Creating the Meeting Place

My meeting place is a very familiar place to me. It is the place where I usually find myself during self-hypnosis or meditation. It came to me years ago, long before I was a hypnotist, during a guided relaxation exercise while doing my masters degree in the UK. It is a place of quiet calm and relaxation, an outdoor pavilion made of white marble. Open on all four sides, it is surrounded by lush green grass, with rolling hills in the distance. It is always sunny with a beautiful blue sky overhead speckled with a few small white, fluffy clouds.

You can enter the pavilion from any side, simply by climbing the three steps that lead from the outside grassy area to the inside. Inside there are small gentle fountains, an in-ground plunge pool, white gauze drapes blowing gently in a soft breeze, and a cool marble floor. Furnished with soft white sofas, white feather pillows, and luxurious down cushions, it has an air of tranquility and spa-like luxury about it. I know from experience that my relaxation space morphs frequently and re-forms according to my unconscious needs and desires. It is a deeply comfortable place for me to explore my unconscious mind with ease.

I decided to visit this space as my place of comfort and, in trance, began to explore the space keeping my mind open that I may find an additional building or room for my CIA to meet. As soon as I entered the white pavilion, I saw that the fountains and plunge pool had disappeared. In their place was a low rectangular table with four white sofas, one on each side.

I sat at one of the sofas and knew that this was indeed the right place for us to meet as a council.

Meeting the Members and Introducing Them to the Chamber

A few days after deciding upon my council, it was time to introduce the members to the space and get to know them each a little better. I took myself into trance and went to my white pavilion. One by one I called each member to mind. This was not the moment to introduce them all to each other, but it was time for us to meet individually. After each meeting, I brought myself out of trance and recorded my findings.

Shawn Carson

I asked Shawn to come to the meeting place. I watched as his familiar form walked up the steps to the main platform, his silver hair shining in the sun. I thanked him for agreeing to join my team and said I had selected him as he fulfilled everything I am looking for in an ally and supporter in writing this book. Shawn has written and published many books, and he is known in the field. He is a creative genius, his mind brimming with ideas and connections. He is also superproductive, having the ability to sit each day and focus on writing, rarely if ever experiencing writer block, and has the ability to organize his thoughts into clear and concise writing. And he is one of the funniest people I know! I asked Shawn if this space was a good space for him and me to meet and discuss our journey together. He shrugged, and in his usual nonchalant manner said sure and promptly took his computer out of his backpack, sat down at a small desk which had just appeared in the corner, and set to work writing.

Stephen King

Next, I asked Stephen King to join me at the white pavilion. I watched as he climbed the steps. I greeted him with a big smile and a handshake. It felt normal and natural to be meeting with him. Out in the real conscious-mind world, I am pretty sure that if I were to meet someone of his stature, I would be somewhat nervous and a bit overwhelmed with the idea of meeting and chatting with a famous person. However, in my inner world, I was calm, collected, and excited to be meeting him. I thanked him for joining my team and asked if this was a good place for us to meet.

"Oh, no, I can't work here," he replied.

I was a little taken aback at his forthrightness and a bit speechless for the briefest of moments until I realized that my unconscious mind could create absolutely anywhere for us to meet. I asked Stephen to show me where he would like to meet, and we were immediately transported to a room in a house. I sensed that the house was somewhere rather remote and the room we were in was upstairs in the house. The room itself looked very lived in and comfortable, with a desk and a straight-backed chair facing a large picture window and shelves on the walls containing books. Papers were scattered on the top of the desk; a pale green typewriter occupied most of the desk space.

There was a steaming cup of tea on the side. It felt as though this was Stephen's office space or writing room. I asked him if he had anything he would like to share with me at the very beginning of our journey together and he said, "I have three pieces of advice to give you as you start out. One: keep the faith; two: connect to the *why;* and lastly, remember to always connect with your reader."

I thanked him and said we would be meeting again soon.

Albert Einstein

As I called Albert Einstein to the white pavilion meeting space, I wondered how this particular meeting would go. Albert Einstein was a genius, and I was suddenly concerned that I wouldn't be able to make head nor tail of what he was saying and would embarrass myself by demonstrating such ignorance of his theories and great work.

Einstein climbed the steps, and with a big grin and an outstretched arm, shook my hand and said, "Wonderful to be here. Thank you for inviting me."

I smiled and thanked him for being willing to be part of my inner council and stated that I had asked him to be a part of this experience because of his creativity and ability to truly think "outside of the box." I asked if this space was good for us to meet. He thought for the briefest of moments and smiled. Suddenly, we were in a cozy book-lined room, a library or study. A roaring fire was ablaze in the fireplace. Einstein was seated in a bottle-green leather wing-backed chair by the fire. He was nonchalantly smoking a pipe. Taking the pipe from his mouth, he asked, "Does this bother you?"

"As a matter of fact it does," I replied, rather surprised at my own honesty.

"Oh don't worry," he said smiling. " I have just invented something to take away the smoke."

At this point, I came out of my trance to write down some of these details. As I returned to the trance, Einstein was still sitting in his wing-backed chair reading the newspaper. He looked up and said, "Always read the newspaper. It keeps you current."

Steve Jobs

I asked Steve Jobs to join me on my council because of his ability to be a visionary. I was also keen for him to share his drive and focus.
I have read lots about Steve Jobs, have seen a few movies of his life, and watched clips of him on YouTube in meetings and giving his famous Stanford University commencement address. Yet I still was surprised when I invited him into the council to find us both outside of the white pavilion.

It was a young Steve who appeared, his hair dark almost to his shoulders. He was casually dressed in black jeans and a black T-shirt and was playing with a long blade of grass, rolling it between his fingers and breaking pieces off and discarding them.

He began to lecture me on the benefits of thinking while walking. "This is me at my most creative" he said, "just wandering around in nature and watching how things work." He continued, "The coolest thing is that I can shift where I am at any moment, so I can be in nature or in the middle of a busy city."

As he said this, the scene changed to the bustling streets of a big metropolitan city, probably somewhere like New York. "I love watching people," he said. "Give people what they want even if they don't know that they want it yet," he said with a smile.

I thanked him and said I was looking forward to meeting again soon.

Eleanor Roosevelt

I invited Eleanor Roosevelt to the white pavilion. I noticed as she climbed the steps that the figure I was looking at was black and white. It struck me as slightly unusual although understandable. Every image or picture I recall seeing of Mrs. Roosevelt has been in black and white. I asked if she could change the color, and magically she transformed before my eyes into color. She was wearing a navy blue coat, navy blue hat with pink flowers, and pale blue gloves. On the crook of her arm she carried a black handbag similar to the style my grandmother had, with a clasp on the top. She wore sensible shoes and smelled like lily-of-the-valley perfume.

Mrs. Roosevelt removed her coat and gloves and was wearing a blue and pink floral day dress. She immediately asked, "Is this where you write? Because this is not the right place for you to be writing anything. It's too relaxed."

I was a little startled and smiled and said, "No, I don't write here. This is where we get together as the council, a comfortable place where we can relax, where everyone is equal and we can share ideas and suggestions."

"That's perfect," Eleanor said. "So where do you write?"

"Well I write anywhere I want," I said.

"You don't have an office with a typewriter?" she asked.

"No" I replied. "I have my laptop computer and I use Dragon Dictate on my iPhone."

Eleanor Roosevelt looked at me blankly. She had no idea to what I was referring. I pulled my iPhone out of my pocket, tapped the app for dictation, and showed her how by simply speaking into my phone this particular app will translate my spoken word into written text.

"Well that is truly amazing," she said. "You really can write anywhere and whenever inspiration strikes. However, you still need to have a special *place* in order to write."

I wasn't quite sure what she meant. I assumed she meant a particular room, maybe a personal desk, my own sacred space for writing, or something else.

Mrs. Roosevelt must've read my mind because she immediately said, "It doesn't have to be a physical space, and you need the right space in your mind to write. Once you have that, then everything will be easy."

I understood exactly what she meant although consciously I'm not aware of exactly where that space is.

"Oh, we are going to get this book written so easily, Sarah," said Mrs. Roosevelt.

I smiled and said, "Well, that's the reason I asked you here, to give me the push that I need, the encouragement, the just-do-it-ness to get this book written."

"Then that's what we'll do," replied Eleanor Roosevelt.

I then asked her if the white pavilion was the best place for us to meet. She smiled and said she liked it fine, however, she preferred the drawing room for our private meetings.

As soon as she said this, we were transported to the elegant drawing room where we had taken tea together. This time there were two comfortable sofas and a low table set with tea. Once again, Mrs. Roosevelt was pouring tea from a fine bone china teapot. "Oh, I do love this time of day when I can simply relax, but I always keep it to a strict 15 minutes. Keeping a tight schedule is vitally important," she said to me with a knowing smile.

Victoria Wood

I softened my mind and focused on meeting Victoria Wood and bringing her into the white pavilion. As soon as I brought her into my mind, I found I was not in the white pavilion but in a very comfortable, warm, inviting kitchen somewhere in a London suburb. There was an AGA gas range on one side and a large pine table in the center of the room. Victoria was standing by the kitchen counter pouring water from the kettle into two mugs. She was making tea just how I make tea, with the tea bag in the bottom of the mug. She brought the mugs to the table, sat down, and asked me to sit. On the table was a plate with chocolate hobnobs. Victoria smiled and said, "Don't expect that next time. We will be friends by then. I only give friends biscuits from the packet."

I explained what her role was to be on my council, and she asked, "So what is it about me that you've always liked?"

"To be honest," I said, "I like your songs more than I like your sketches."

"What is it about my songs specifically that you like?" she asked.

"Well, it's your observational humor and your cleverness with words," I replied.

Victoria smiled and said, "That cleverness with words can take a very long time. There's a lot of hard work that goes on behind the scenes."

I nodded knowingly. I have written a few books in the past, and I know that it does take a great deal of time and effort to get a book published. To go from having the thought to writing it down to editing to finally getting a book published.

"Sometimes, I have to take a break from my own writing," she said. "I get way too serious about the comedy, and I have to take a break. I usually watch some other comedians, like Morecombe and Wise, to make me smile, so I understand the need for humor in this process."

As she said this, I knew that she was exactly the right person for the job.

Council Meeting 1

As I opened my mind to setting up the first meeting, I entered my white pavilion. I sat on one sofa, with the entrance steps to the pavilion on my right, and I asked the members of my Inner Council to enter the pavilion and to take a seat. I didn't place them in any particular area or arrange the seating in any way. I simply allowed the members of my council to choose their own seats.

Einstein and Steve Jobs took the sofa to my immediate right, Einstein closest to me. Opposite me at the far end of the coffee table sat Shawn and Stephen King. The two ladies took the sofa on my left, with Eleanor Roosevelt closest to me and Victoria Wood on her left. Interestingly, for many of our subsequent meetings, everyone took the same seats.

I welcomed everyone and thanked them all once again for agreeing to be members of my Council of Inner Advisers, and for their guidance and support for me in the process of writing this book. I then asked everyone to introduce him or herself, starting with Einstein.

Einstein simply smiled at everyone and said, "Hello, I'm Albert Einstein, and I'm here to help Sarah in any way I can. She has asked me specifically to focus on creativity, thinking outside the box, and in generating new and different ideas."

Everyone smiled and nodded.

Steve Jobs then said, "Hi, I'm Steve. Sarah has asked me to be here to help her with focus, although I think I can bring a great deal more to this process than simply that."

I smiled at Shawn next, and he said, "I'm here to help Sarah just get this book done."

I smiled, recognizing Shawn's "straight-to-the-pointed-ness."

Stephen King was next and he said, "Thank you, Sarah, for inviting me to this council. I can bring a wealth of experience, as I have spent my entire life writing even before I knew I was a writer."

I smiled and thanked him.

Victoria Wood then took the floor and said, "Hullo" in a strong British Northern accent. "I'm here to have fun, to help Sarah to have fun, and we can all have fun in this process, can't we?"

I smiled and nodded and noticed that everyone else was smiling and agreeing too.

Just as Eleanor Roosevelt was about to speak, Einstein interjected and said, "Oh, here comes bossy boots."

To which Eleanor replied, "No, not to you, Mr. Einstein, only to Sarah. She is the one we are all here for after all. It is my role to motivate her and to ensure that she has the correct incentive to get this book written."

Mr. Einstein smiled and nodded and said, "Yes, that's what we're here for. I was just having a bit of fun!"

I then thanked everyone for introducing him or herself and said that we would undoubtedly enjoy working together as a team. I explained again that we would meet sometimes as an entire group, possibly in small groups, or even individually, and that at this point, I was uncertain as to exactly how we would meet. I asked if everyone was comfortable with having a very flexible schedule, and everyone agreed. I then asked everyone to give me one piece of advice, one tidbit, one takeaway for me as I was starting out in this writing process. We went around the group in the same order, starting with Einstein.

Instantly, we were all in an old, beautiful, high-ceiling library. The kind of library you might see in a stately home, with shelves of books reaching from floor to ceiling, comfortable chairs arranged around the room, and ladders attached to the walls to slide easily from one shelf to another.

"I have brought you here for a reason," said Einstein. "Each and every one of these books was written by someone. These books are filled with someone's ideas, thoughts, stories, theories, so precious to them they wanted to share them with the world. Each and every one of these writers had their own method of writing, their own process and went through their own struggles. Some of these books were written very easily, the words flowing from mind to page. Some authors probably struggled to get the words down, and their books may have taken years to write. Each author went through a period of transformation; each one broke their own rules. So I say to you, Sarah, as my piece of advice: break your own rules."

I wasn't certain exactly what Einstein meant by this, but I trusted that my unconscious mind would make sense of it.

Suddenly, we were back in the white pavilion sitting around the coffee table. Steve Jobs pulled out an iPhone, held it up, and said to everyone, "This is my library. Remember that the readers of today read books on these devises, and the readers of tomorrow will access books in ways we haven't even begun to think about yet. My advice to you is to keep your eye on the prize and set yourself targets that you can easily reach. Oh, and one more thing: each day set yourself a target that you can't reach."

I thanked Steve and asked Shawn for his advice. In typical Shawn fashion, he simply said, "Just write, just write something, just start, and the rest will flow easily." I smiled having heard this advice from Shawn before I knew he was absolutely right.

I turned to Stephen King and asked him for his nugget of advice. He smiled and said, "Keep your reader in mind." Short and simple and absolutely true.

I then asked Victoria Wood for her advice as I started out on this new project. She smiled and said, "Smile often when you're writing." This seemed to make perfect sense to me because I know that when we smile our brain releases dopamine. This is a feel-good neurotransmitter and feeling good while writing is a wonderful thing.

Finally, I asked Eleanor Roosevelt for her piece of wisdom. She said, "A little every day." Short and sweet.

I thanked everyone for their advice, knowing that I would take this forward as I began the process of writing.

Council Meeting 2

I went into trance and took myself to the white pavilion. All the members of my council were already seated. I explained that the purpose of bringing the council together today was that I had a certain question that I wanted to pose to the council. I explained that I had been going back and forth about the structure of the book, in particular where and how to place my experience of using a CIA Council to write the book. I knew I had a number of options, and I was curious to know what the council members thought about where I should place the telling of my story. I didn't share my own opinions or even explain the different options that I had come up with; I just opened the question up to the council members and asked them to share their ideas, one person at a time, as where they thought the best place for the story would be.

Einstein was the first to comment. He said, "I think the entire story should be at the very end of the book, maybe an appendix or even a final chapter. This way your experience won't interfere with the reader's experience."

Steve Jobs then chimed in, "Well, you can do both, at the end of each individual chapter and a complete story at the end of the book. So, for example, at the end of the "Choosing Your Council" chapter, you would insert the section of your story on how you chose your council and the same for the "Using Your Council" and other chapters. Then at the end of the entire book, you could lay out your entire story so that those people who wish to have some guidance can have that on their way through, and people can also read it as one entire process."

I thanked Steve for his input and asked Shawn for his thoughts. Shawn has written many books, writes very quickly, and has a really good sense of making the structure of the book clear and easy for the readers to understand. Shawn shrugged his shoulders, smiled, and said, "Either way works for me. I think it's a good idea to include your story, but I really don't mind how you include it."

Stephen King raised his hand next and said he would like to make some comments. "As a storywriter," he said, "it's important to lead the reader on throughout the story, to give them something to hold onto, to spark their imagination so that they are continually curious and always wanting to find out the next part of the story."

Victoria Wood nodded in agreement and said, "As a comedian who had a long career," she said, "I have scripted many performances, and it's the same thing in my line of work too. I have to give the audience a little bit of something first almost to entice them into a small giggle or a little smile before I can deliver the punch line, so I think it's a really good idea to lead your reader through the process as they go through."

Stephen King smiled in agreement.

The others listened patiently as I asked Eleanor Roosevelt what her opinion was. She shrugged and said, "Either way is absolutely fine, just as long as you just get this book written."

I smiled to myself and thought, "Yep, I should have known she would say something like that. After all, that is the job I've given her, and she herself said that she was like a dog with a bone, and now she is determined to motivate me to get this book written."

At this point, I asked the council members to move their seats so they sat with somebody who is aligned with their own opinion. Shawn and Eleanor Roosevelt had said that either way is absolutely fine for them, so they sat on a double sofa on my left. Victoria Wood and Stephen King had both expressed interest in sharing the story throughout the book, almost as a real-life explanation for each chapter, so I asked them to sit on the double sofa opposite me. Steve Jobs and Einstein had both, at some point, talked about having an additional chapter, so I asked them to sit in the double sofa to my right. I asked Einstein to sit closer to me and Steve Jobs to sit closer to Stephen King and Victoria Wood, as he really was the balance between those two options. Asking people to move their seat helped me to mentally organize everyone's opinion.

Once everybody had moved into the new seating arrangement, it was very clear that the majority of people were saying that I should have pieces of my experience throughout the book. Shawn and Eleanor Roosevelt were more neutral. Stephen King, Victoria Woods, and Steve Jobs liked the idea of using the personal experience throughout. That left only Albert Einstein with a strong opinion of leaving my entire story right to the end. As his opinion differed so strongly to the others, I asked him once again to explain further as to why he thought this was the best route.

Einstein thought for a moment, taking his time to consider what he wanted to say, and when he spoke, he smiled at Stephen King and Victoria Wood and said, "Your experiences are fantastic and are both based on storytelling and entertainment. Sarah is writing a very different book. This is an informational guide, a how-to, a nonfiction book."

He then proceeded to ask the entire council, "What is the purpose of this book? I'll tell you. I believe this book is meant to teach people, to give them the skills so they can eventually have their own experience. If Sarah shares her story all the way through, isn't she influencing the reader's experience? As the reader reads the book, they will be having their own personal unconscious experience whether they realize it or not. Some parts of the brain will be playing with these ideas, trying on these thoughts, creating their own council members, and experiencing in their own unique and individual way. This is the point of this entire book. Will the reader unconsciously or even consciously copy Sarah's experience?"

As he spoke, I saw many of the other members nodding in agreement.

Shawn then said, "You are absolutely right, Professor Einstein. We are influencing the reader's unconscious mind. But I think we have to give even more credit to our readers and realize that if Sarah shares her story through the book, we are simply drawing guidelines, laying out the plan, giving the scaffolding so that the reader will fill in their own experience. And by sharing her story, isn't Sarah making the process easier for the reader to have their own experience?"

Again members nodded in agreement.

At this point, Einstein pointed out the white flowers in a vase on the table between us. I had not been aware of them until this moment. Einstein said, "Take some time to smell the roses," and smiled at me. He continued: "Make this experience as multisensory as possible."

The unconscious mind often gives images and symbols, and I have learned over the years to simply acknowledge and accept anything that happens during trance. So I smiled and took note of the roses and the message, knowing that my unconscious mind was doing something that I was not entirely aware of!

"Oh, and by the way, make sure you write everything down," Einstein added.

I realized that we had been talking extensively for quite some time. The council had shared lots of ideas, and it was important for me to step out of the meeting to write down everything about my experience. I asked the council to excuse me for a while and that I would return and, if necessary, we would continue our discussion at a later time.

Private Meetings with Stephen King and Shawn Carson

I had another question about the structure of the book, in particular whether to include only my experience of writing the book or experiences that other people have had with their CIA Councils. I decided to ask for a private meeting with Stephen King and then for a private meeting with Shawn. I selected these two members of my council to meet with privately because they are both published authors and both experienced in structuring books.

I took myself into trance and found myself sitting on the white sofa in my white pavilion. While sitting on my sofa in the white pavilion, I found myself going into trance. A trance within a trance! It was an unusual experience, and I experienced a very deep trance.

I met Stephen King in his office space, the upstairs room of the rural house. There was a sofa, its back towards the window, and Stephen's writing desk behind us. The space was very lived in and slightly messy, giving a comfortable sense to the room. Stephen invited me to sit down on the sofa, and I asked my question: "Stephen, should I include just my experience throughout the book or include those of others?"

Stephen said, "As long as you make it very clear whose experience you are writing about it will be fine. In my books, I have many characters, many threads, many plot lines, and the secret is to keep them separate and as clear as possible so the reader can follow along. Of course, in my books, many of these characters and plot lines cross and become intertwined. However, it is important, particularly at the beginning, to draw clear distinctions. Hope this helps."

I came out of trance briefly to record this meeting.

I then took myself back into trance and to my white pavilion. I saw Shawn writing at his desk in the corner, and I went inside. A chair materialized next to him, and I sat down. Shawn looked up from his writing and said, "What's up?"

I asked the same question: "Should I include just my experience or include those of other clients?"

Shawn smiled and said, "Well, you won't know until you try. I would suggest including yours and others and then seeing how it all fits together."

I thanked Shawn and brought myself out of trance.

Council Meeting 3

I went into trance just before falling asleep and called a brief meeting of the council. I explained that I was doing well with writing the book and simply wanted a word of encouragement from each of the members.

Eleanor Roosevelt went first and said, "Fortitude."

Victoria Wood smiled and said, "Mr. Rotivator." (There was a comedy sketch years ago in the UK where two older ladies talk about a TV fitness instructor nicknamed Mr. Motivator. In the sketch, the two ladies call him Mr. Rotivator. This sketch always made me giggle.)

Stephen King simply said, " Strength."

Shawn said, "Moving."

Steve Jobs made a "whooosh" sound, and moved his hand in a forward motion.

Einstein nodded and said, "Understanding."

I thanked everyone, took a moment to write these words down, and drifted off to sleep.

Council Meeting 4

I took myself into trance and then to my white pavilion. The council members were already seated in their usual seats. I thanked them for their help thus far in writing this book and explained that I felt I was at a crucial point in my writing. I had written more than 20,000 words and hoped I was about halfway through. I wanted to maintain the motivation, direction, and focus necessary to complete the book in a timely manner. I explained that I would ask each member to provide me with a symbol or an object to help motivate me, sharpen my focus, and keep me on track.

I asked Stephen King first, and he immediately gave me a small golden anchor. It looked like a charm for a bracelet or possibly a pendant from a necklace. I thanked him and placed it on the table before me. Shawn then gave me a muffin in a colorful purple wrapper. It looked a dark color, possibly a whole wheat or chocolate muffin. Once again, I thanked him and turned to Steve Jobs. He gave me the blade of grass that he had been playing with when we first met in the meadow outside the white pavilion. Einstein then gave me a ball of energy. It appeared almost as a hologram of white and yellow light between his hands. Eleanor Roosevelt gave me a small glass thimble. Victoria Wood gave me a black beret.

I took some time to examine the six items on the table in front of me. I then took each object one by one and asked my unconscious mind to provide me with some deeper understanding as to the meaning of the symbol. I was well aware that the unconscious mind may or may not provide me with an explanation for the symbol. I was comfortable with that.

I took the golden anchor in my hand and instantly had an understanding of anchoring myself to the outcome. I took the muffin into myself symbolically. It felt comfortable; however, I found no further meaning. I held the blade of grass in my hand and allowed that to give me its meaning. Instantly, I heard Steve Jobs saying, "Every tiny thing is important; every blade of grass has its worth." I placed my hands around the ball of energy and instantly felt its meaning. It was the sense of pure potentiality. I held the small glass thimble in my hand and was somewhat curious as to what the meaning may be. A thimble seems a very old-fashioned tool, and I don't think I've ever seen a glass thimble in the real world. However, as soon as I picked it up, I could hear Eleanor Roosevelt saying something about it being a sign of a woman working hard, and the fact that it was glass represented beauty. As I looked at the black beret that Victoria Wood gave me, it immediately brought a smile to my face. "That's what it's for," quipped Victoria instantly, "to make you smile." (One of her most famous comedy characters often wore a beret, and this represented continuing to have fun and to smile through the process.)

I then took all the objects into myself, into my heart, my soul, and my being, knowing that my unconscious mind would make even more meaning from these items as I moved forward with the writing of this book.

Council Meeting 5

I wanted to meet with my council to ask for their opinion on the color for the book cover. I went into trance, entered the white pavilion, and watched as everyone entered. The first figure to enter was unfamiliar to me. He was wearing a white floppy hat, was in his 40s, and had shoulder-length black hair and a droopy mustache. He was carrying an easel, paint, and paintbrushes.

I said, "Hello."

He said, "Hello. I understand you are talking about color today?"

I nodded, and he extended his hand to shake mine and introduced himself. "Hello, I'm Gauguin."

I smiled and welcomed him to the council chamber.

By then, the other members of the council were arriving, and there was a definite shift in the atmosphere. Einstein was wearing an old-fashioned painter's smock and a large black bow at the neck. He was carrying a painting palette and was flamboyantly waving paintbrushes around while declaring, "I'm ready!"

People were giggling and laughing as they entered. Eleanor Roosevelt had more flowers in her hat than usual.

Victoria Wood was dressed in a long yellow-ish overcoat and was wearing her beret. She said, "I went to a nude drawing class once, but I didn't realize I was supposed to wear clothes." Everyone roared with laughter.

Steve Jobs and Stephen King were slapping each other on the back and laughing with Shawn about something. It was a substantially different atmosphere and feeling than we had ever experienced before in our council meetings. There was an air of expectancy, of fun, of playfulness. It was wonderful.

Everyone settled into their usual seats, and Gauguin set up his easel at the corner between two sofas. He said he was going to paint us all having our meeting. I called the meeting to order and explained that I would like suggestions and ideas for the cover color. The CIA Pattern book was to be part of our NLP Mastery Series. All the books in this series have a compass symbol on the front and a specific color. We already had turquoise, orange, apple green, and pinkish red. We were also about to publish another book that would be purple, so these colors and shades were off the table.

I asked each person to let me know what colors they thought would be best for the book.

Eleanor Roosevelt began and said she thought navy blue would be the best color. "It is always practical to have things in navy blue. It goes with everything," she said.

I thanked her and asked Victoria Wood. "Yellow," she said. "Absolutely. Yellow."

I turned to Stephen King, and he said, "Blood red," with a wicked smirk on his face.

I then asked Shawn, and he said, "I don't really mind as long as we stick with the same theme of the compass and a color."

Steve Jobs said, "Packaging is absolutely essential, and I like neutrality and quality. I think it would be amazing to have this book in black and gray."

Lastly I turned to Albert Einstein, and he said, "I see it in my mind's eye a royal blue color."

I thanked everyone and then asked Gauguin to show us the picture. He had painted us all in his usual Tahitian style with bright colors and surrounded by tropical fruits. We all roared with laughter again. I thanked everyone for coming and asked each one to leave a copy of the book on the seat as they left.

I wanted to do the "to-sit-in-my-chair" exercise. In this exercise, I sit in each person's chair and take on his or her perspective and point of view and look at the book cover each had suggested.

I moved to Eleanor Roosevelt's chair and picked up the copy of the book. It had a navy blue front cover that felt rather mundane and dull. I put the book down and moved to Victoria Wood's chair. I picked up the yellow book and, interestingly enough, the title changed to a book I hoped to write in the future! From here, I moved to Stephen King's seat and held the blood red book. I liked the dynamic impact of this book. I moved to Shawn's seat, and here the book I picked up changed into a wide variety of colors and did not settle on one in particular. As soon as I sat in Steve Jobs's seat and picked up the black-and-gray book, I knew instantly that it didn't work for me. The last seat was Albert Einstein's. I saw the royal blue cover of the book and liked it instantly.

I decided to allow my unconscious mind, through sleep incubation, to process the discussion and decide what should be which color the book.

That night before going to sleep, I took myself into trance and asked my unconscious mind to make the decision. I remember waking in the night and seeing what I can only describe as "peacock" colors in my mind's eye.

The next morning I remembered waking and thinking about the peacock color. I realized that a peacock is comprised of purples and blues and greens. Although this gave me the spectrum that I was most comfortable with, it did not settle on one specific color.

The next evening I had a strong and complex dream that involved cutting open a melon. As soon as the melon was cut open, it was a bright blue inside.

Upon waking and writing down my dreams, I realized that this was the right color for the front cover of this book.

Council Meeting 6

I went into trance and took myself to my meeting place, the white pavilion. It was dark and stormy outside and raining quite hard. I did not know if this had any meaning. I noted it because I am aware that in the world of trance, everything has some kind of symbolic meaning.

One by one members entered. Eleanor Roosevelt was first to come in, followed by Victoria Wood, who shook the rain out of her umbrella and placed it by her side. Einstein came in taking off a raincoat and asked if there was somewhere for him to hang it up. As if by magic, a coat stand appeared, and Einstein hung his coat and sat down. Stephen King, Shawn, and Steve Jobs all rushed in, trying to avoid the rain.

I thanked everyone for meeting and explained that I have a certain question or dilemma and wished to use the Polar Sphinx Pattern to help solve this issue. The interesting fact is that the dilemma is around where to place the Polar Sphinx Pattern within the book.

I explained that the Polar Sphinx Pattern involves two members of my council who hold different and opposing views on the subject and that I would select two members to take part in this pattern while the remaining members would be free to leave.

I explained to the council that I was uncertain whether to keep the Polar Sphinx Pattern as its own individual chapter or include it in the "Interacting with Your Council" chapter. I asked if any of the council members have strong opinions about this.

Eleanor Roosevelt said, "Yes, I think it should be it's own standalone chapter."

Steve Jobs immediately jumped in and said, "Well, I'm not so sure. I think it should be part of the "Interacting with Your Council" chapter.

My two council members for the Polar Sphinx Pattern had self-selected. I thanked them and asked if they were willing to work with me on this pattern. They both agreed. I then asked the other members of my council to leave. The other members of the council simply faded away taking with them the hat stand, coats, and umbrellas and leaving Eleanor, Steve, and me in the white pavilion.

I asked Eleanor and Steve to remain seated in their usual places, and I sat in my usual seat. Interestingly, the weather had now cleared. It was bright and sunny with a blue sky. I explained that I would ask each person to put forward his or her point of view, without interruption.

Eleanor spoke first: "I think the Polar Sphinx Pattern should be its own individual chapter. It is a clear pattern for solving issues and dilemmas and deserves a full chapter. You are using this specific pattern to help you write the book and will undoubtedly include a transcript of this very meeting."

Steve said, "Well, I think we have to consider the difference between the "Interacting with Your Council" chapter and the chapters that explain individual patterns. It seems to me that the exercises and suggestions included in the "Interacting with Your Counsel" chapter offer suggestions of how to interact with your council members at different times while the individual chapters are opportunities to step inside each individual council member, to get to know them more deeply. These individual chapters also lay out how to utilize the changes in a more traditional hypnotic or NLP sense. I think this particular pattern is more about the interaction with the council as opposed to a traditional NLP pattern."

I thanked them both for the points of view, and we moved into the Sphinx part of this pattern.

I asked them to then stand up and to switch places. I watched as Eleanor walked around the sofas to sit in Steve's seat and Steve walked to sit in the place where Eleanor usually sits.

As soon as Eleanor Roosevelt sat down in Steve Jobs's chair, I noticed a shift in her physiology. Her head tilted to one side, and she looked very thoughtful for a moment. I asked her how she felt. She responded that although she still felt that the pattern deserved its own chapter, she could see that it also could have a place in the "Interacting with Your Council" chapter. It really could be in either or both.

I turned to Steve Jobs and asked what he felt. He replied that he still felt that it should be included in the "Interacting with Your Council" chapter because he didn't see that it was as NLP-like as the New Behavior Generator, the BEAT Pattern, or the Perfect Coach Pattern. I asked him if he felt it offered more insight into the council members, and he said, "Yes, to a point. The other patterns ask the client to step into the council members, and this one is purely observational."

I could see just how focused and stubborn Steve Jobs was about this, and that gave me more insight into his character!

I thanked both Eleanor and Steve for joining me in this process and offering me even more insight and perspective.

Even though this particular interaction did not offer me the answer or solution. It did give me more to think about and helped me to make my final decision.

Appendix Two: Shawn's Original Council of Advisers

For the sake of completeness, we set out below thumbnail sketches of the members of Shawn's original Council of Invisible Advisers.

Shawn subsequently gathered other CIA groups for specific projects. For example: when co-writing the book *Deep Trance Identification* with Jess Marion and John Overdurf, Shawn convened a master mind CIA consisting of Vladimir Raikov (the "father" of DTI), John Overdurf (who was also a cowriter but lives in Atlanta and Scottsdale so was not always available "live"), Steve Jobs and Thomas Edison (two people Shawn did extensive DTI work with), and Constantin Stanislavski (the "father" of method acting whose tools are used extensively in the DTI book).

During this work, Shawn had a number of dream encounters with Stanislavski, some of which are described in the book *Deep Trance Identification*. Stanislavski and Steve Jobs have since become active members of Shawn's CIA on an ongoing basis.

Hannibal of Carthage

This bold and daring general is a bitter enemy of Rome. At a time in Rome's history, when Rome's armies are unbeatable on land (Carthage is a naval power, but not a military power), Hannibal recruits and marches a ragtag army through the length of Spain and the width of France; marches his army, which includes a number of elephants, across the Alps; and brilliantly defeats every army that Rome sends against him. The only reason Rome does not fall to this inspirational and brilliant general is that Hannibal does not have the siege weapons necessary to successfully besiege Rome. Nevertheless, Hannibal's army marches at will up and down the length of Italy whilst Rome's vaunted legions cower behind the defensive walls of Rome.

Richard Feynman

This brilliant scientist and Nobel Prize winner is known as one of the "fathers" of quantum physics, itself probably the most revolutionary scientific theory ever developed. He develops the pictorial representation of the basic building blocks of the universe. These representations are called Feynman diagrams. He also helped to develop the atomic bomb and is appointed to the panel that investigated the space shuttle *Challenger* disaster. But Professor Feynman is much more than this. He is also a lock picker, drum player, magician, and educator who could make the most complex topic in quantum physics easily accessible to his first-year physics class. He has a unique combination of practical understanding leading to insightful abstractions to fundamental principles, a sense of humor that makes him a practical joker, a highly developed moral sense, and an IQ that is simply off the charts.

Wolfgang Amadeus Mozart

This child prodigy goes on to become one of the most famous composers of all time. But that is not why he is on the list. Rather, it is Mozart's ability to absorb the influences of others and to combine those influences into his own unique style, his ability to think visually about an auditory discipline, and his ability to pour his passion into his work and hence write music at an incredible rate. In addition, his lavish dress sense, obscene humor, and quirky personality add a touch of color to the Council of Advisers. He is a creative artist.

John Overdurf

As the best NLP trainer on the planet, John is a natural choice for the council. John is a master of NLP and hypnosis; as such, he excels in getting the best out of those around him. His principal skills are calibration and his ability to elicit states in others.

Sherlock Holmes

This master detective roams the streets of Victorian London solving crime and bringing criminals to justice. He does not do so out of a strong sense of justice (although he has this). Rather, he fights crime because he believes that this is the area where he could best exercise his amazing mental powers. His principal skill is observation. He observes the smallest detail of human behavior and draws inferences therefrom. He also draws from a vast reservoir of knowledge on any and all subjects relevant to his passion. He is a man of action and takes to the streets to find the information he needs. He is socially introverted, which leads to some strange passions, such as playing the violin, engaging in indoor target practice, and, on occasion, taking opium. He is a master observer.

Don Juan Matus

Don Juan Matus is the teacher and mentor of Carlos Castaneda. Don Juan inhabits a world radically different than that of most human beings. He brings third attention to his experience of the universe and, therefore, sees energy for what it is. He is not fooled by the normalizations that most of humanity lives by.

Although bringing a unique perspective to the council, Don Juan also brings a wicked sense of humor, teasing those around him until their mental constructions collapse. Don Juan is a sorcerer and a warrior.

Margaret Thatcher

Margaret Thatcher was the Prime Minister of the UK at a critical time in the country's history. She took power when the country had lost its self-respect and was plagued by strike after strike. Mrs. Thatcher came to power with a fierce determination to follow her own agenda and to get things done. This determination won her the title of the "Iron Lady." She famously used the phrase "The lady is not for turning" during a speech dismissing critics who suggested she change course. Mrs. Thatcher is a determined leader.

Leonardo da Vinci

Leonardo is the Renaissance man, scientist, artist, and thinker. His vision stretches to what may be possible, and reaches way beyond "what might be possible given certain limitations which may apply." Many of his inventions—such as the helicopter and submarine—could be constructed centuries after his death only when engineering caught up with his amazing dreams. Leonardo achieves this by connecting ideas from diverse fields. By doing so, he thinks in radically new and creative ways. He is *the* Renaissance Man.

Bruce Lee

Although known as an action movie star, Bruce is actually first a totally original thinker who happens to use his talents in the area of the martial arts. Like Leonardo, Bruce is able to synthesize ideas from different disciplines. In Bruce's case, however, the disciplines are all related; they are all martial arts. By capturing the best ideas from each of these disciplines, Bruce has constructed a martial art radically different from anything that previously existed, and in many ways more effective than other martial arts that have been developed over centuries. The result of Bruce's involvement in the martial arts is a quantum leap in knowledge, and one could reasonably ascribe to Bruce the credit for modern martial arts. As a result of this, Bruce also brings an amazing knowledge of the human body as a tool. Bruce is human physical potential personified.

Tony Stark

Tony Stark—engineer, inventor, entrepreneur, and playboy—is best known as Ironman. Tony has turned his knowledge and engineering skill into a superhuman superhero. His real skill is turning an idea into reality, a real complement to Leonardo's dreaming. Tony Stark simply is Ironman!

Other Books In This Series

The Swish
By Shawn Carson and Jess Marion

The Visual Squash
By Jess Marion and Shawn Carson

The Meta Pattern
By Shawn and Sarah Carson

The BEAT Pattern
By Shawn and Sarah Carson

Conversational Regression
By Jess Marion

Other Books By This Publisher

Deep Trance Identification: Unconscious Modeling and Mastery for Hypnosis Practitioners, Coaches, and Everyday People
By Shawn Carson and Jess Marion with John Overdurf

Deep Trance Identification Companion
By Shawn Carson and Jess Marion with John Overdurf

Quit: The Hypnotist's Handbook to Running Effective Stop Smoking Sessions
By Jess Marion, Sarah Carson, and Shawn Carson

Keeping the Brain in Mind: Practical Neuroscience for Coaches, Therapists, and Hypnosis Practitioners
By Shawn Carson and Melissa Tiers

Tree of Life Coaching: Practical Secrets of the Kabbalah for Hypnosis and NLP Practitioners and Coaches
By Shawn Carson

I Quit: Stop Smoking Easily Through the Power of Hypnosis
By Jess Marion, Sarah Carson, and Shawn Carson

From Call to Client
By Jess Marion, Sarah Carson, and Shawn Carson

HypnoGames for HypnoJunkies
By Sarah Carson, Shawn Carson, and Jess Marion

Small Thoughts for Big Change: 21 Beliefs to Create Magic in Your Life
By Sarah Carson, Shawn Carson, and Jess Marion

The Reality Distortion Field: Change the World by Convincing Others to Share Your Dreams
By Shawn Carson

Have Mercy: 21 Tales to Trance-Form Your Life
By Mercedes Herman

Printed in Great Britain
by Amazon

17034546R00108